BALED HAY

LECTOR HOUSE PUBLIC DOMAIN WORKS

BALED HAY

BILL NYE

ISBN: 978-93-90058-99-0

Published: 1884

© 2020
LECTOR HOUSE LLP

LECTOR HOUSE LLP
E-MAIL: lectorpublishing@gmail.com

BALED HAY

A DRIER BOOK THAN
WALT WHITMAN'S "LEAVES O' GRASS."

BY

BILL NYE

Author of "Bill Nye and Boomerang," "Forty Liars and Other Lies,"
"Goose-Neck Smith," "How Came Your Eye Out, and
Your Nose Not Skun?" Etc., Etc., Etc.

Heap cold day when Melican man no lite em blook.

—AH SIN.

ILLUSTRATED BY
F. OPPER, OF "PUCK"

1884

DEDICATION.

TO MY WIFE:

Who has courteously and heroically laughed at my feeble
and emaciated jokes, even when she did not feel like it;
who has again and again started up and agitated
successfully the flagging and reluctant applause,
who has courageously held my coat through
this trying ordeal, and who, even now, as
I write this, is in the front yard warning
people to keep off the premises until
I have another lucid interval,

This Volume is Affectionately Inscribed,

By The

AUTHOR.

PIAZZA TO THE THIRD VOLUME.

There can really be no excuse for this last book of trite and beautiful sayings. I do not attempt, in any way, to palliate this great wrong. I would not do so even if I had an idea what palliate meant.

It will, however, add one more to the series of books for which I am to blame, and the pleasure of travel will be very much enhanced, for me, at least.

There is one friend I always meet on the trains when I travel. He is the news agent. He comes to me with my own books in his arms, and tells me over and over again of their merits. He means it, too. What object could he have in coming to me, not knowing who I am, and telling me of their great worth? Why would he talk that way to me if he did not really feel it?

That is one reason I travel so much. When 1 get gloomy and heartsick, I like to get on a train and be assured once more, by a total stranger, that my books have never been successfully imitated.

Some authors like to have a tall man, with a glazed grip-sack, and whose breath is stronger than his intellect, selling their works; but I do not prefer that way.

I like the candor and ingenuousness of the train-boy. He does not come to the front door while you are at prayers, and ring the bell till the hat-rack falls down, and then try to sell you a book containing 2,000 receipts for the blind staggers. He leans gently over you as you look out the car window, and he puts some pecan meats in your hand, and thus wins your trusting heart. Then he sells you a book, and takes an interest in you.

This book will go to swell the newsboy's armful, and if there be any excuse, under the sun, for its publication, aside from the royalty; that is it.

I have taken great care to thoroughly eradicate anything that would have the appearance of poetry in this work, and there is not a thought or suggestion contained in it that would soil the most delicate fabric.

Do not read it all at once, however, in order to see whether he married the girl or not. Take a little at a time, and it will cure gloom on the "*similia simili-bus curanter*" principle. If you read it all at once, and it gives you the heaves, I am glad of it, and you deserve it. I will not bind myself to write the obituary of such people.

B.N.

Hudson, Wis., Sept, 5,1883.

CONTENTS

CONTENTS

LIST OF ILLUSTRATIONS

BALED HAY

A NOVEL NOVELETTE.

I NEVER wrote a novel, because I always thought it required more of a mashed-rasp-berry imagination than I could muster, but I was the business manager, once, for a year and a half, of a little two-bit novelette that has never been published.

I now propose to publish it, because I cannot keep it to myself any longer.

Allow me, therefore, to reminisce.

Harry Bevans was an old schoolmate of mine in the days of and although Bevans was not his sure-enough name, it will answer for the purposes herein set forth. At the time of which I now speak he was more bashful than a book agent, and was trying to promote a cream-colored mustache and buff "Donegals" on the side.

Suffice it to say that he was madly in love with Fanny Buttonhook, and too bashful to say so by telephone.

Her name wasn't Buttonhook, but I will admit it for the sake of argument. Harry lived over at Kalamazoo, we will say, and Fanny at Oshkosh. These were not the exact names of the towns, but I desire to bewilder the public a little in order to avoid any harassing disclosures in the future. It is always well enough, I find, to deal gently will those who are alive and moderately muscular.

Young Bevans was not specially afraid of old man Buttonhook, or his wife. He didn't dread the enraged parent worth a cent. He wasn't afraid of anybody under the cerulean dome, in fact, except Miss Buttonhook; but when she sailed down the main street, Harry lowered his colors and dodged into the first place he found open, whether it was a millinery store or a livery stable.

Once, in an unguarded moment, he passed so near her that the gentle south wind caught up the cherry ribbon that Miss Buttonhook wore at her throat, and slapped Mr. Bevans across the cheek with it before he knew what ailed him. There was a little vision of straw hat, brown hair, and pink-and-white cuticle, as it were, a delicate odor of violets, the "swish" of a summer silk, and my friend, Mr. Bevans, put his hand to his head, like a man who has a sun-stroke, and fell into a drug store and a state of wild mash, ruin and helpless chaos.

His bashfulness was not seated nor chronic. It was the varioloid, and didn't hurt him only when Miss Buttonhook was present, or in sight. He was polite and chatty with other girls, and even dared to be blithe and gay sometimes, too, but when Frances loomed up in the distance, he would climb a rail fence nine feet high to evade her.

He told me once that he wished I would erect the frame-work of a letter to Fanny, in which he desired to ask that he might open up a correspondence with her. He would copy and mail it, he said, and he was sure that I, being a disinterested party, would be perfectly calm.

I wrote a letter for him, of which I was moderately proud. It would melt the point on a lightning rod, it seemed to me, for it was just as full of gentleness and poetic soothe as it could be, and Tupper, Webster's Dictionary and my scrap-book had to give down first rate. Still it was manly and square-toed. It was another man's confession, and I made it bulge out with frankness and candor.

As luck would have it, I went over to Oshkosh about the time Harry's prize epistle reached that metropolis, and having been a confidant of Miss B's from early childhood, I had the pleasure of reading Bev's letter, and advising the young lady about the correspondence.

Finally a bright thought struck her. She went over to an easy chair, and sat down on her foot, coolly proposing that I should outline a letter replying to Harry's, in a reserved and rather frigid manner, yet bidding him dare to hope that if his orthography and punctuation continued correct, he might write occasionally, though it must be considered entirely *sub rosa* and abnormally *entre nous* on account of "Pa."

By the way, "Pa" was a druggist, and one of the salts of the earth—Epsom salts, of course.

I agreed to write the letter, swore never to reveal the secret workings of the order, the grips, explanations, passwords and signals, and then wrote her a nice, demure, startled-fawn letter, as brief as the collar to a party dress, and as solemn as the Declaration of Independence.

Then I said good-by, and returned to my own home, which was neither in Kalamazoo nor Oshkosh. There I received a flat letter from 'William Henry Bevans, inclosing one from Fanny, and asking for suggestions as to a reply. Her letter was in Miss Buttonhook's best vein. I remember having written it myself.

Well, to cut a long story short, every other week I wrote a letter for Fanny, and on intervening weeks I wrote one for the lover at Kalamazoo. By keeping copies of all letters written, I had a record showing where I was, and avoided saying the same pleasant things twice.

Thus the short, sweet summer scooted past. The weeks were filled with gladness, and their memory even now comes back to me, like a wood-violet-scented vision. A wood-violet-scented vision comes high, but it is necessary in this place.

Toward winter the correspondence grew a little tedious, owing to the fact that I had a large, and tropical boil on the back of my neck, which refused to declare its intentions or come to a focus for three weeks. In looking over the letters of both lovers yesterday, I could tell by the tone of each just where this boil began to grow up, as it were, between two fond hearts.

This feeling grew till the middle of December, when there was a red-hot quarrel. It was exciting and spirited, and after I had alternately flattered myself first from Kalamazoo and then from Oshkosh, it was a genuine luxury to have a row with myself through the medium of the United States mails.

Then I made up and got reconciled. I thought it would be best to secure harmony before the holidays so that Harry could go over to Oshkosh and spend Christmas. I therefore wrote a letter for Harry in which he said he had, no doubt, been hasty, and he was sorry. It should not occur again. The days had been like weary ages since their quarrel, he said—vicariously, of course—and the light had been shut out of his erstwhile joyous life. Death would be a luxury unless she forgave him, and Hades would be one long, sweet picnic and lawn festival unless she blessed him with her smile.

You can judge how an old newspaper reporter, with a scarlet imagination, would naturally dash the color into another man's picture of humility and woe.

She replied—by proxy—that he was not to blame. It was her waspish temper and cruel thoughtlessness. She wished he would come over and take dinner with them on Christmas day and she would tell him how sorry she was. When the man admits that he's a brute and the woman says she's sorry, it behooves the eagle eye of the casual spectator to look up into the blue sky for a quarter of an hour, till the reconciliation has had a chance and the brute has been given time to wipe a damp sob from his coat-collar.

I was invited to the Christmas dinner. As a successful reversible amanuensis I thought I deserved it. I was proud and happy. I had passed through a lover's quarrel and sailed in with whitewinged peace on time, and now I reckoned that the second joint, with an irregular fragment of cranberry jelly, and some of the dressing, and a little of the white meat please, was nothing more than right.

Mr. Bevans forgot to be bashful twice during the day, and even smiled once also. He began to get acquainted with Fanny after dinner, and praised her beautiful letters. She blushed clear up under her "wave," and returned the compliment.

That was natural. When he praised her letters I did not wonder, and when she praised his I admitted that she was eminently correct. I never witnessed better taste on the part of two young and trusting hearts.

After Christmas I thought they would both feel like buying a manual and doing their own writing, but they did not dare to do so evidently. They seemed to be afraid the change would be detected, so I piloted them into the middle of the succeeding fall, and then introduced the crisis into both their lives.

It was a success.

I felt about as well as though I were to be cut down myself, and married off in the very prime of life. Fanny wore the usual clothing adopted by young ladies who are about to be sacrificed to a great horrid man. I cannot give the exact description of her trousseau, but she looked like a hazel-eyed angel, with a freckle on the bridge of her nose. The groom looked a little scared, and moved his gloved hands as though they weighed twenty-one pounds apiece.

However, it's all over now. I was up there recently to see them. They are quite happy. Not too happy, but just happy enough. They call their oldest son Birdie. I wanted them to call him William, but they were headstrong and named him Birdie. That wounded my pride, and so I called him Earlie Birdie.

GREELEY AID RUM.

WHEN I visit Greeley I am asked over and over again as to the practical workings of woman suffrage in Wyoming, and when I go back to Wyoming I am asked how prohibition works practically in Greeley, Col. By telling varied and pleasing lies about both I manage to have a good deal of fun, and also keep the two elements on the anxious seat.

There are two sides to both questions, and some day when I get time and have convalesced a little more, I am going to write a large book relating to these two matters. At present I just want to say a word about the colony which bears the name of the Tribune philosopher, and nestles so lovingly at the chilly feet of the Rocky mountains. As I write, Greeley is apparently an oasis in the desert. It looks like a fertile island dropped down from heaven in a boundless stretch of buffalo grass, sage hens and cunning little prairie dogs. And yet you could not come here as a stranger, and within the colonial barbed wire fence, procure a bite of cold rum if you were President of the United States, with a rattlesnake bite as large as an Easter egg concealed about your person. You can, however, become acquainted, if you are of a social nature and keep your eyes open.

I do not say this because I have been thirsty these few past weeks and just dropped on the game, as Aristotle would say, but just to prove that men are like boys, and when you tell them they can't have any particular thing, that is the thing they are apt to desire with a feverish yearn. That is why the thirstful man in Maine drinks from the gas fixture; why the Kansas drinkist gets his out of a rain-water barrel, and why other miracles too numerous to mention are performed.

Whisky is more bulky and annoying to carry about in the coat-tail pocket than a plug of tobacco, but there have been cases where it was successfully done. I was shown yesterday a little corner that would hold six or eight bushels. It was in the wash-room of a hotel, and was about half full. So were the men who came there, for before night the entire place was filled with empty whisky bottles of every size, shape and smell. The little fat bottle with the odor of gin and livery stable was there, and the large flat bottle that you get at Evans, four miles away, generally filled with something that tastes like tincture of capsicum, spirits of ammonia and lingering death, is also represented in this great congress of cosmopolitan bottles sucked dry and the cork gnawed half up.

When I came to Greeley, I was still following the course of treatment prescribed by my Laramie City physician, and with the rest, I was required to force down three adult doses of brandy per day. He used to taste the prescription at times to see if it had been properly compounded. Shortly after my arrival here I ran out of this remedy and asked a friend to go and get the bottle refilled. He was a man not familiar with Greeley in its moisture-producing capacity, and he was unable to procure the vile demon in the town for love or wealth. The druggist even did not keep it, and although he met crowds of men with tears in their eyes and breath like a veteran bung-starter, he had to go to Evans for the required opiate. This I use externally, now, on the vagrant dog who comes to me to be fondled and who goes away with his hair off. Central Colorado is full of partially bald dogs who have wiped their wet, cold noses on me, not wisely but too well.

ABOUT SAW MILLS.

RIVER FALLS, WIS., MAY 80.

I HAVE just returned from a trip up the North Wisconsin railway, where I went to catch a string of codfish, and anything else that might be contagious. The trip was a pleasant one and productive of great good in many ways. I am hardening myself to railway traveling, like Timberline Jones' man, so that I can stand the return journey to Laramie in July.

Northern Wisconsin is the place where the "foreign lumber" comes from which we use in Laramie in the erection of our palatial residences. I visited the mill last week that furnished the lumber used in the Oasis hotel at Greeley. They yank a big wet log into that mill and turn it into cash as quick as a railroad man can draw his salary out of the pay car. The log is held on a carriage by means of iron dogs while it is being worked into lumber. These iron dogs are not like those we see on the front steps of a brown stone house occasionally. They are another breed of dogs.

The managing editor of the mill lays out the log in his mind, and works it into dimension stuff, shingle holts, slabs, edgings, two by fours, two by eights, two by sixes, etc., so as to use the goods to the best advantage, just as a woman takes a dress pattern and cuts it so she won't have to piece the front breadths, and will still have enough left to make a polonaise for the last-summer gown.

I stood there for a long time watching the various saws and listening to their monotonous growl, and wishing that I had been born a successful timber thief instead of a poor boy without a rag to my back.

At one of these mills, not long ago, a man backed up to get away from the carriage, and thoughtlessly backed against a large saw that was revolving at the rate of about 200 times a minute. The saw took a large chew of tobacco from the plug he had in his pistol pocket, and then began on him.

But there's no use going into details. Such things are not cheerful. They gathered him up out of the sawdust and put him in a nail keg and carried him away, but he did not speak again. Life was quite extinct. Whether it was the nervous shock that killed him, or the concussion of the cold saw against his liver that killed him, no one ever knew.

The mill shut down a couple of hours so that the head sawyer could file his saw, and then work was resumed once more.

"THEY PUT HIM IN A NAIL-KEG AND CARRIED HIM AWAY."

A sad funeral procession.

We should learn from this never to lean on the buzz saw when it moveth itself aright.

EXPERIMENTS WITH OLD CHEESE.

A RECENT article in a dairy paper is entitled, "Experiments with Old Cheese." We have experimented some on the venerable cheese, too. One plan is to administer chloroform first, then perform the operation while the cheese is under its influence. This renders the experiment entirely painless, and at the same time it is more apt to keep quiet. After the operation the cheese may be driven a few miles in the open air, which will do away with the effects of the chloroform.

THE RAG-CARPET.

WITH the threatened eruption of the rag carpet as a kind of venerable successor to the genuine Boston-made Turkish rug, there comes a wail on the part of the male portion of humanity, and a protest on the part of all health-loving humanity.

I rise at this moment as the self-appointed representative of poor, down-trodden and long-suffering man. Already lady friends are looking with avaricious and covetous eyes on my spring suit, and, in fancy, constructing a stripe of navy blue, while some other man's spring clothes are already spotted for the "hit-or-miss" stripe of this time-honored humbug.

It does seem to me that there is enough sorrowing toil going for nothing already; enough of back ache and delirium, without tearing the shirts off a man's back to sew into a big ball, and then weave into a rag carpet made to breathe death and disease, with its prehistoric perspiration and its modern drug store dyes.

The rug now commonly known as the Turkish prayer rug, has a sad, worn look, but it does not come up to the rag carpet of the dear old home.

Around it there clusters, perhaps, a tradition of an Oriental falsehood, but the rag carpet of the dear old home, rich in association, is an heir-loom that passes down from generation to generation, like the horse blanket of forgotten years or the ragbag of the dear, dead past. Here is found the stripe of all-wool delaine that was worn by one who is now in the golden hence, or, stricken with the Dakota fever, living in the squatter's home; and there is the fragment of underclothes prematurely jerked from the back of the husband and father before the silver of a century had crept into his hair. There is no question but the dear old rag carpet, with poisonous greens and sickly yellows and brindle browns and doubtful blacks, is a big thing. It looks kind of modest and unpretending, and yet speaks of the dead past, and smells of the antique and the garret.

It represents the long months when aching fingers first sewed the garments, then the first dash of gravy on the front breadth, the maddening cry, the wild effort to efface it with benzine, the sorrowful defeat, the dusty grease-spot standing like a pork-gravy plaque upon the face of the past, the glad relinquishment of the garment, the attack of the rag-carpet fiend upon it, the hurried crash as it was torn into shreds and sewn together, then the mad plunge of the dust-powdered mass into the reeking bath of Paris green or copperas, then the weaver's gentle racket, and at last the pale, consumptive, freckled, sickly panorama of outrageous coloring, offending the eye, the nose, the thorax and the larynx, to be trodden under feet of men, and to yield up its precious dose of destroying poisons from generation even unto generation.

It is not a thing of beauty, for it looks like the colored engraving of a mortified lung. It is not economical, for the same time devoted to knocking out the brains of frogs and collecting their hams for the metropolitan market would yield infinitely more; and it is not worth much as an heirloom, for within the same time a mortgage may be placed upon the old homestead which will pass down from father to son, even to nations yet unborn, and attract more attention in the courts than all the rag carpets that it would require to span the broad, spangled dome of heaven.

I often wonder that Oscar Wilde, the pale patron of the good, the true and the beautiful, did not rise in his might and knock the essential warp and filling out of the rag carpet. Oscar did not do right, or he would have stood up in his funny clothes and fought for reform at so much per fight. While he made fun of the Chicago water works, a grateful public would have buried him in cut flowers if, instead, he had warped it to the rag carpet and the approaching dude.

A TRYING SITUATION.

THERE are a great many things in life which go to atone for the disappointments and sorrows which one meets," but when a young man's rival takes the fair Matilda to see the baseball game, and sits under an umbrella beside her, and is at the height of enjoyment, and gets the benefit of a "hot ball" in the pit of his stomach, there is a nameless joy settles down in the heart of the lonesome young man, such as the world can neither give nor take away.

ONE KIND OF A BOY.

I AM always sorry to see a youth get irritated and pack up his clothes, in the heat of debate, and leave the home nest. His future is a little doubtful, and it is hard to prognosticate whether he will fracture limestone for the streets of a great city, or become President of the United States; but there is a beautiful and luminous life ahead of him in comparison with that of the boy who obstinately refuses to leave the home nest.

The boy who cannot summon the moral courage some day to uncoil the tendrils of his heart from the clustering idols of the household, to grapple with outrageous fortune, ought to be taken by the ear and led away out into the great untried realm of space.

While the great world throbs on, he sighs and refuses to throb. While other young men put on their seal-brown overalls and wrench the laurel wreath and other vegetables from cruel fate, the youth who dangles near the old nest, and eats the hard-earned groceries of his father, shivers on the brink of life's great current and sheds the scalding tear.

He is the young-man-afraid-of-the-sawbuck, the human being with the unlaundried spinal column. The only vital question that may be said to agitate his pseudo brain is, whether he shall marry and bring his wife to the home nest, or marry and tear loose from his parents to live with his father-in-law. Finally he settles it and compromises by living alternately with each.

How the old folks yearn to see him. How their aged eyes light up when he comes with his growing family to devour everything in sight and yawn through the space between meals. This is the heyday of his life; the high noon of the boy who never ventured to ride the yearling colt, or to be yanked through the shimmering sunlight at the tail of a two-year-old. He never dared to have any fun because he might bump his nose and make it bleed on his clean clothes. He never surreptitiously cut the copper wire off the lightning rod to snare suckers with, and he never went in swimming because the great, rude boys might duck him or paint him with mud. He shunned the green apple of boyhood, and did not slide down hill because he would have to pull his sled back to the top again.

Now, he borrows other people's newspapers, eats the provisions of others, and sits on the counter of the grocery till the proprietor calls him a counter irritant.

There can be nothing more un-American than this flabby polyp, this one-horse tadpole that never becomes a frog. The average American would rather burst up in business six times in four years, and settle for nine cents on the dollar, than to lead such a life. He would rather be an active bankrupt than a weak and bilious barnacle on the clam-shell of home.

The true American would rather work himself into luxury or the lunatic asylum than to hang like a great wart upon the face of nature. This young man is not in accordance with the Yankee schedule, and yet I do not want to say that he belongs to any other nation. Foreign powers may have been wrong; trans-Atlantic nations may have erred, and the system of European government may have been erroneous, but I would not come out and charge them with this horrible responsibility. They never harmed me, and I will not tarnish their fair fame with this grave indictment.

He will breathe a certain amount of atmosphere, and absorb a given amount of feed for a few years, and then the full-grown biped will leave the home nest at last. The undertaker will come and get him and take what there is left of him out to the cemetery. That will be all. There can be no deep abiding sorrow for him here; public buildings will not be draped in mourning, and you can get your mail at the usual hour when he dies. The band will not play a sadder strain because the fag-end of a human failure has tapered down to death, and the soft and shapeless features are still. You will have no trouble getting a draft cashed on that day, and the giddy throng will join the picnic as they had made arrangements to do.

THE CHAMPION MEAN MAN.

LARAMIE has the champion mean man. He has a Sunday handkerchief made to order with scarlet spots on it, which he sticks up to his nose just before the plate starts round, and leaves the church like a house on fire. So after he has squeezed out the usual amount of gospel, he slips around the corner and goes home ten cents ahead, and has his self-adjusting nose-bleed handkerchief for another trip.

FRATERNAL SPARRING.

I HAVE just returned from a little two-handed tournament with the gloves. I have filled my nose with cotton waste so that I shall not soak this sketch in gore as I write.

I needed a little healthful exercise and was looking for something that would be full of vigorous enthusiasm, and at the same time promote the healthful flow of blood to the muscles. This was rather difficult. I tried most everything, but failed. Being a sociable being (joke) I wanted other people to help me exercise, or go along with me when I exercised. Some men can go away to a desert isle and have fun with dumb-bells and a horizontal bar, but to me it would seem dull and commonplace after a while, and I would yearn for more humanity.

Two of us finally concluded to play billiards; but we were only amateurs and the owner intimated that he would want the table for Fourth of July, so we broke off in the middle of the first game and I paid for it.

Then a younger brother said he had a set of boxing-gloves in his room, and although I was the taller and had longer arms, he would hold up as long its he could., and I might hammer him until I gained strength and finally got well.

I accepted this offer because I had often regretted that I had not made myself familiar with this art, and also because I knew it would create a thrill of interest and fire me with ambition, and that's what a hollow-eyed invalid needs to put him on the road to recovery.

The boxing-glove is a large fat mitten, with an abnormal thumb and a string at the wrist by which you tie it on, so that when you feed it to your adversary he cannot swallow it and choke himself. I had never seen any boxing-gloves before, but my brother said they were soft and wouldn't hurt anybody. So we took off some of our raiment and put them on. Then we shook hands. I can remember distinctly yet that we shook hands. That was to show that we were friendly and would not slay each other.

My brother is a great deal younger than I am and so I warned him not to get excited and come for me with anything that would look like wild and ungovernable fury, because I might, in the heat of debate, pile his jaw up on his forehead and fill his ear full of sore thumb. He said that was all right and he would try to be cool and collected.

Then we put our right toes together and I told him to be on his guard. At that moment I dealt him a terrific blow aimed at his nose, but through a clerical error of mine it went over his shoulder and spent itself in the wall of the room, shattering a small holly-wood bracket, for which I paid him $3.75 afterward. I did not wish to buy the bracket because I had two at home, but he was arbitrary about it and I bought it.

We then took another athletic posture, and in two seconds the air was full of poulticed thumb and buckskin mitten. I soon detected a chance to put one in where my brother could smell of it, but I never knew just where it struck, for at that moment I ran up against something with the pit of my stomach that made me throw up the sponge along with some other groceries, the names of which I cannot now recall.

My brother then proposed that we take off the gloves, but I thought I had not sufficiently punished him, and that another round would complete the conquest, which was then almost within my grasp. I took a bismuth powder and squared myself, but in warding off a left-hander, I forgot about my adversary's right and ran my nose into the middle of his boxing-glove. Fearing that I had injured him, I retreated rapidly on my elbows and shoulder-blades to the corner of the room, thus giving him ample time to recover. By this means my younger brother's features were saved, and are to-day as symmetrical as my own.

I can still cough up pieces of boxing-gloves, and when I close my eyes I can see calcium lights and blue phosphorescent gleams across the horizon; but I am thoroughly convinced that there is no physical exercise which yields the same amount of health and elastic vigor to the puncher that the manly art does. To the punchee, also, it affords a large wad of glad surprises and nose bleed, which cannot be hurtful to those who hanker for the pleasing nervous shock, the spinal jar and the pyrotechnic concussion.

That is why I shall continue the exercises after I have practiced with a mule or a cow-catcher two or three weeks, and feel a little more confidence in myself.

CHIPETA'S ADDRESS TO THE UTES.

PEOPLE of my tribe! the sorrowing widow of the dead Ouray speaks to you. She comes to you, not as the squaw of the dead chieftain, to rouse you to war and victory, but to weep with you over the loss of her people and the greed of the pale face.

The fair Colorado, over whose Rocky mountains we have roamed and hunted in the olden time, is now overrun by the silver-plated Senator and the soft-eyed dude.

We are driven to a small corner of the earth to die, while the oppressor digs gopher holes in the green grass and sells them to the speculator of the great cities toward the rising sun.

Through the long, cold winter my people have passed, in want and cold, while the conqueror of the peaceful Ute has worn $250 night-shirts and filled his pale skin with pie.

Chipeta addresses you as the weeping squaw of a great man whose bones will one day nourish the cucumber vine. Ouray now sleeps beneath the brown grass of the canyon, where the soft spring winds may stir the dead leaves, and the young coyote may come and monkey o'er his grave. Ouray was ignorant in the ways of the pale face. He could not go to Congress, for he was not a citizen of the United States. He had not taken out his second papers. He was a simple child of the forest, but he stuck to Chipeta. He loved Chipeta like a hired man. That is why the widowed squaw weeps over him.

A few more years and I shall join Ouray—my chief, Ouray the big Injun from away up the gulch. His heart is still open to me. Chipeta could trust him, even among tire smiling maidens of her tribe. Ouray was true. There was no funny business in his nature. He loved not the garb of the pale face, but won my heart while he wore a saddle-blanket and a look of woe.

Chipeta looks to the north and the south, and all about are the graves of her people. The refinement of the oppressor has come, with its divorce and schools and gin cocktails and flour bread and fall elections, and we linger here like a boil on the neck of a fat man.

Even while I talk to you, the damp winds of April are sighing through my vertebras, and I've got more pains in my back than a conservatory.

Weep with the widowed Chipeta. Bow your heads and howl, for our harps are hung on the willows and our wild goose is cooked.

Who will be left to mourn at Chipeta's grave? None but the starving pappooses of my nation. We stand in the gray mist of spring like dead burdocks in the field of the honest farmer, and the chilly winds of departing winter make us hump and gather like a burnt boot.

All we can do is to wail. We are the red-skinned wailers from Wailtown.

Colorado is no more the home of the Ute. It is the dwelling place of the bonanza Senator, who doesn't know the difference between the plan of salvation and the previous question.

Chipeta cannot vote. Chipeta cannot pay taxes to a great nation, but you will be apt to hear her gentle voice, and her mellow racket will fill the air till her tongue is cold, and they tuck the buffalo robe about her and plant her by the side of her dead chieftain, where the south wind and the sage hen are singing.

BILL NYE'S CAT.

(By Permission.)

BILL NYE'S CAT.

(BY PERMISSION.)

I AM not fond of cats, as a general rule. I never yearned to have one around the house. My idea always was, that I could have trouble enough in a legitimate way without adding a cat to my woes. With a belligerent cook and a communistic laundress, it seems to me most anybody ought to be unhappy enough without a cat.

I never owned one until a tramp cat came to our house one day during the present autumn, and tearfully asked to be loved. He didn't have anything in his make-up that was calculated to win anybody's love, but he seemed contented with a little affection,—one ear was gone and his tail was bald for six inches at the end, and he was otherwise well calculated to win confidence and sympathy. Though we could not be madly in love with him, we decided to be friends, and give him a chance to win the general respect.

Everything would have turned out all right if the bobtail waif had not been a little given to investigation. He wanted to know more about the great world in which he lived, so he began by inspecting my house. He got into the store-room closet and found a place where the carpenter had not completed his job. This is a feature of the Laramie artisan's style. He leaves little places in unobserved corners generally, so that he can come back some day and finish it at an additional cost of fifty dollars. This cat observed that he could enter at this point and go all over the imposing structure between the flooring and the ceiling. He proceeded to do so.

We will now suppose that a period of two days has passed. The wide halls and spacious façades of the Nye mansion are still. The lights in the banquet-hall are extinguished, and the ice-cream freezer is hushed to rest in the wood-sned. A soft and tearful yowl, deepened into a regular ring-tail-peeler, splits the solemn night in twain. Nobody seemed to know where it came from.

I rose softly and went to where the sound had seemed to well up from. It was not there.

I stood on a piece of cracker in the diningroom a moment, waiting for it to come again. This time it came from the boudoir of our French artist in soup-bone symphonies and pie—Mademoiselle Bridget O'Dooley. I went there and opened the door softly, so as to let the cat out without disturbing the giant mind-that had worn itself out during the day in the kitchen, bestowing a dry shampoo to the china.

Then I changed my mind and came out. Several articles of vertu, beside Bridget, followed me with some degree of vigor.

The next time the tramp cat yowled he seemed to be in the recesses of the bath-room. I went down stairs and investigated. In doing so I drove my superior toe into my foot, out of sight, with a door that I encountered. My wife joined me in the search. She could not do much, but she aided me a thousand times by her counsel. If it had not been for her mature advice I might have lost much of the invigorating exercise of that memorable night.

Toward morning we discovered that the cat was between the floor of the children's play-room and the ceiling of the dining-room. We tried till daylight to persuade the cat to come out and get acquainted, but he would not.

At last we decided that the quickest way to get the poor little thing out was to let him die in there, and then we could tear up that portion of the house and get him out. While he lived we couldn't keep him still long enough to tear a hole in the house and get at him.

It was a little unpleasant for a day or two waiting for death to come to his relief, for he seemed to die hard, but at last the unearthly midnight yowl was still. The plaintive little voice ceased to vibrate on the still and pulseless air. Later, we found, however, that he was not dead. In a lucid interval he had discovered the hole in the store-room where he entered, and, as we found afterward a gallon of coal-oil spilled in a barrel of cut loaf-sugar, we concluded that he had escaped by that route.

That was the only time that I ever kept a cat, and I didn't do it then because I was suffering for something to fondle. I've got a good deal of surplus affection, I know, but I don't have to spread it out over a stump-tail orphan cat.

AUTUMN THOUGHTS.

IN the Rocky mountains now the eternal whiteness is stealing down toward the foot-hills and the brown mantle of October hangs softly on the swelling divide, while along the winding streams, cottonwood and willow are turned to gold, and the deep green of the solemn pines lies farther back against the soft blue of the autumn sky. The sigh of the approaching storm is heard at eventide, and the hostile Indian comes into the reservation to get some arnica for his chilblain, and to heal up the old feeling of intolerance on the part, of the pale face.

He leaves the glorious picture of mountain and glen; the wide sweep of magnificent nature, where a thousand gorgeous dyes are spread over the remains of the dead summer, and folding his tepee, he steals into the home of the white man that he may be once more at peace with the world.

The hectic of the dying year saddens and depresses him, for is it not an emblem to him of the death of his race? Is it not to him an assurance that in the golden ultimately, the red man will be sought for on the face of the earth and he will not be able to represent. He will not be there either in person or by proxy. Here and there may be found the little silent mounds with some glass beads and teeth in them, but the silent warrior with the Roman nose will not be there.

The Indian agent will have a large, conservative cemetery on his hands, and the brave warrior will be marching single file through the corridors of the hence.

At this moment he does not look romantic. Clothed in a coffee sack and a little brief authority, he would not make a good vignette on a $5 bill. His wife, too, looks careworn, and the old glad light is not in her eye. Pier gunny-sack dolman is not what it once was, and her beautifully arched foot has spread out over the reservation more than it used to. Her step has lost its old elasticity, and so have her suspenders.

Autumn brings to her nothing but regret for the past and hopelessness for the future. The cold and cruel winter will bring her nothing but bitter memories and condemned government grub. The solemn hush of nature and the gorgeous coloring of the forest do not awake a thrill in her wild heart. She cares not for the dead summer or the mellow mist of the grand old mountains.

She doesn't care two cents. She knows that no sealskin sacque will come to her on the Christmas trees, and the glad welcome of the placid and select oyster is not for her.

"AT THIS MOMENT HE DOES NOT LOOK ROMANTIC,"

Is it surprising, then, that to this decaying belle of an old family the sparkle of hope is unknown? Can we wonder, as we contemplate her history, that to her the soldier pantaloons of last year, and the bullwhacker's straw hat of '79, are obnoxious?

She is like her sex, and her joy is fractured by the knowledge that her moccasins are down at the heel, and her stockings existing in the realms of fancy. We should not look with scorn upon Mrs. Rise-up-William-Riley, for hope is dead in her breast, and the wigwam is desolate in the sage-brush.

Daughter of a great nation, we are not mad at you. You are not to be blamed because the republican party has busted your crust. We do not hate you because you eat your steak-rare and wear your own hair. It is your own right to do so if you wish. Brace up, therefore, and take a tumble, as it were, and try to be cheerful. We will not massacre you if you will not massacre us. All we want is peace, and you can wear what you like, only wear something, if you please, when you come into our society. We do not ask you to conform strictly to our false and peculiar costumes, but wear something to protect you from the chilling blasts of winter and you will win our respect. You needn't mingle in our society much if you do not choose to, but wrap yourself up in most any kind of clothing that will silence the tongue of slander, and try to quit drinking. You would get along first-rate if you would only let liquor alone. Do not try to drown your sorrows in the flowing bowl. It's expensive and unsatisfactory. Take our advice and swear off. We have tried it, and we know what we are talking about.

You have a glorious future before you, if you will cease to drink the vintage of the pale face, and monkey with petty larceny. Look at Pocahontas and Mrs. Tecumseh. They didn't drink. They were women of no more ability than you have, but they were high-toned, and they got there, Eli. Now they are known to history along with Cornwallis and Payne. You can do the same if you choose to. Do not be content to lead a yellow dog around by a string and get inebriated, but rise up out of the alkali dust, and resolve that you will shun the demon of drink.

You ought to be ashamed of yourself.

THE MAN WHO INTERRUPTS.

I DO not, as a rule, thirst for the blood of my fellow-man. I am willing that the law should in all ordinary cases take its course, but when we begin to discuss the man who breaks into a conversation and ruins it with his own irrelevant ideas, regardless of the feelings of humanity, I am not a law and order man. The spirit of the "Red Vigilanter" is roused in my breast and I hunger for the blood of that man.

Interrupters are of two classes: First, the common plug who thinks aloud, and whose conversation wanders with his so-called mind. He breaks into the saddest and sweetest of sentiment, and the choicest and most tearful of pathos, with the remorseless ignorance that marks a stump-tail cow in a dahlia bed. He is the bull in my china shop, the wormwood in my wine, and the kerosene in my maple syrup. I am shy in conversation, and my unfettered flights of poesy and sentiment are rare, but this man is always near to mar all with a remark, or a marginal note, or a story or a bit of politics, ready to bust my beautiful dream and make me wish that his name might be carved on a marble slab in some quiet cemetery, far away.

Dear reader, did you ever meet this man—or his wife? Did you ever strike some beautiful thought and begin to reel it off to your friends only to be shut off in the middle of a sentence by this choice and banner idiot of conversation? If so, come and sit by me, and you may pour your woes into my ear, and I in turn will pour a few gallons into your listening ear.

I do not care to talk more than my share of the time, but I would be glad to arrive at a conclusion just to see how it would seem. I would be so pleased and so joyous to follow up an anecdote till I had reached the "nub," as it were, to chase argument home to conviction, and to clinch assertion with authority and evidence.

The second class of interrupters is even worse. It consists of the man—and, I am pained to state, his wife also—who see the general drift of your remarks and finish out your story, your gem of thought or your argument. It is very seldom that they do this as you would do it yourself, but they are kind and thoughtful and their services are always at hand. No matter how busy they may be, they will leave their own work and fly to your aid. With the light of sympathy in their eyes, they rush into the conversation, and, partaking of your own zeal, they take the words from your mouth, and cheerfully suck the juice out of your joke, handing back the rind and hoping for reward. That is where they get left, so far as I am concerned. I am almost always ready to repay rudeness with rudeness, and cold preserved gall with such acrid sarcasm as I may be able to secure at the moment. No one will ever know how I yearn for the blood of the interrupter. At night I camp on his trail, and all the day I thirst for his warm life's current. In my dreams I am cutting his scalp loose with a case-knife, while my fingers are twined in his clustering hair. I walk over him and promenade across his abdomen as I slumber. I hear his ribs crack, and I see his tongue hang over his shoulder as he smiles death's mirthful smile.

I do not interrupt a man no more than I would tell him he lied. I give him a chance to win applause or decomposed eggs from the audience, according to what he has to say, and according to the profundity of his profund. All I want is a similar chance and room according to my strength. Common decency ought to govern conversation without its being necessary to hire an umpire armed with a four-foot club, to announce who is at the bat and who is on deck.

It is only once in a week or two that the angel troubles the waters and stirs up the depths of my conversational powers, and then the chances are that some leprous old nasty toad who has been hanging on the brink of decent society for two weeks, slides in with a low kerplunk, and my fair blossom of thought that has been trying for weeks to bloom, withers and goes to seed, while the man with the chilled steel and copper-riveted brow, and a wad of self-esteem on his intellectual balcony as big as an inkstand, walks slowly away to think of some other dazzling gem, and thus be ready to bust my beautiful phantom, and tear out my high-priced bulbs of fancy the next time I open my mouth.

THE ROCKY MOUKTAIN COW.

THE attention of the Rocky Mountain Detective Association is respectfully called to a large bay cow, who is hanging around this place under an assumed name. She has no visible means of support, and has been seen trying to catch the combination to the safes of several of our business men here. She has also stolen into our lot several times and eaten two or three lengths of stovepipe that we neglected to lock up.

PRESERVING EGGS.

THE Scientific American gives this as an excellent mode of preserving eggs: "Take fresh, ones, put a dozen or more into a small willow basket, and immerse this for five seconds in boiling water, containing about five pounds of common brown sugar per gallon, then pack, when cool, small ends down, in an intimate mixture of one part of finely powdered charcoal and two of dry bran. In this way they will last six months or more. The scalding water causes the formation of a thin skin of hard albumen near the inner surface of the shell, and the sugar of syrup closes all the pores."

The Scientific American neglects, however, to add that when you open them six months after they were picked and preserved, the safest way is to open them out in the alley with a revolver, at sixteen paces. When you have succeeded in opening one, you can jump on a fleet horse and get out of the country before the nut brown flavor catches up with you.

HUMAN' NATURE ON THE HALF-SHELL.

I AM up here in River Falls, Wisconsin, and patiently waiting for the snowbanks to wilt away and gentle spring to come again. Gentle spring, as I go to press, hath not yet loomed up. Nothing in fact hath loomed up, as yet, save the great Dakota boom. Everybody, from the servant girl with the symphony in smut on her face and the boundless waste of freckles athwart her nose, up to the normal school graduate, with enough knowledge to start a grist mill for the gods, has "a claim" in the promised land, the great wild goose orchard and tadpole aquarium of the new Northwest.

The honest farmer deserts his farm, around which clusters a thousand memories of the past, and buckling on his web feet, he flees to the frog ponds of the great northern watershed, to make a "tree claim," and be happy.

Such is life. We battle on bravely for years, cutting out white-oak grubs, and squashing army worms on a shingle, in order that we may dwell beneath our own vine and plum tree, and then we sell and take wings toward a wild, unknown country, where land is dirt cheap, where the wicked cease from troubling and the weary are at rest.

That is where we get left, if I may be allowed an Americanism, or whatever it is. We are never at rest. The more we emigrate the more worthless, unsatisfied and trifling we become. I have seen the same family go through Laramie City six times because they knew not of contentment. The first time they went west in a Pullman car "for their health." The husband rashly told a sad-eyed man that he lied, and in a little while the sun was obscured by loose teeth and hair. The ground was torn up and vegetation was killed where the discussion was held.

Then the family went home to Toledo. They went in a day coach and said a Pullman car was full of malaria and death. Their relatives made sport of them and lifted up their yawp and yawped at them insomuch that the yawpness thereof was as the town caucus for might. Then the tourists on the following spring packed up two pillows, and a pink comforter, and a change of raiment, and gat them onto the emigrant train and journeyed into the land which is called Arizona, where the tarantula climbeth up on the innerside of the pantaloon and tickleth the limb of the pilgrim as he journeyeth, and behold he getteth in his work, and the leg of that man is greater than it was aforetime, even like unto the leg of a piano.

A FRIGID ROUTE.

THERE'S no doubt but that the Fort Collins route to the North Park, is a good, practicable route, but the only man who has started out over it this spring fetched up in the New Jerusalem.

The trouble with that line of travel is, that the temperature is too short. The summer on the Fort Collins route is noted mainly for its brevity. It lasts about as long as an ordinary eclipse of the sun.

The man who undertook to go over the road this spring on snow shoes, with a load consisting of ten cents' worth of fine cut tobacco, has not been heard from yet at either end of the line, and he is supposed to have perished, or else he is still in search of an open polar sea.

It is hoped that dog days will bring him to the surface, but if the winter comes on as early this fall as there are grave reasons to fear, a man couldn't get over the divide in the short space of time which will intervene between Decoration day and Christmas.

We hate to discourage people who have an idea of going over the Fort Collins road to North Park, but would suggest that preparations be made in advance for about five hundred St. Bernard dogs and a large supply of arctic whisky, to be placed on file where it can be got at without a moment's delay.

TOO CONTIGUOUS.

THERE is a firm on Coyote creek, in New Jersey, that would like to advertise in *The Boomerang*, and the members of the firm are evidently good square men, although they are not large. They lack about four feet in stature of being large enough to come within the range of our vision.

They have got more pure gall to the superficial foot than anybody we ever heard of. It seems that the house has a lot of vermifuge to feed plants, and a bedbug tonic that it wants to bring before the public, and it wants us to devote a quarter of a column every day to the merits of these bug and worm discouragers, and then take our pay out of tickets in the drawing of a brindle dog next spring.

We might as well come right out end state that we are not publishing this paper for our health, nor because we like to loll around in luxury all day in the voluptuous office of the staff. We have mercenary motives, and we can't work off wheezy parlor organs and patent corn plasters and threshing machines very well. We desire the scads. We can use them in our business, and we are gathering them in just as fast as we can. At the present time we are pretty well supplied with rectangular churns and stem-winding mouse traps. We do not need them, It takes too much time to hypothecate them.

In closing, we will add, that New Jersey people will not be charged much more for advertising space than Wyoming people. We have made special rates so that we can give the patrons of the East almost as good terms as our home advertisers.

THE AMENDE HONORABLE.

IT is rather interesting to watch the manner by which old customs have been slightly changed and handed down from age to age. Peculiarities of old traditions still linger among us, and are forked over to posterity like a wappy-jawed teapot or a long-time mortgage.. No one can explain it, but the fact still remains patent that some of the oddities of our ancestors continue to appear from time to time, clothed in the changing costumes of the prevailing fashion.

Along with these choice antiquities, and carrying the nut-brown flavor of the dead and relentless years, comes the amende honorable. From the original amende in which the offender appeared in public clothed only in a cotton-flannel shirt, and with a rope about his neck as an evidence a formal recantation, down to this day when (sometimes) the pale editor, in a stickful of type, admits that "his informant was in error," the amende honorable has marched along with the easy tread of time. The blue-eyed moulder of public opinion, with one suspender hanging down at his side, and writing on a sheet of news-copy paper, has a more extensive costume, perhaps, than the old-time offender who bowed in the dust in the midst of the great populace, and with a halter under his ear admitted his offense, but he does not feel any more cheerful over it.

I have been called upon several times to make the amende honorable, and I admit that it is not an occasion of mirth and merriment. People who come into the editorial office to invest in a retraction are generally very healthy, and have a stiff, reserved manner that no cheerfulness of hospitality can soften..

I remember of an accident of this kind which occurred last summer in my office, while I was writing something scathing. A large map with an air of profound perspiration about him, and a plaid flannel shirt, stepped into the middle of the room, and breathed in the air that I was not using. He said he would give me four minutes in which to retract, and pulled out a watch by which to ascertain the exact time.

I asked him if he would not allow me a moment or two to go over to the telegraph office and to wire my parents of my awful death. He said I could walk out of that door when I walked over his dead body. Then I waited a long time, until he told me my time was up, and asked what I was waiting for. I told him I was waiting for him to die, so that I could walk over his dead body. How could I walk over a corpse until life was extinct?

"HE SAID HE WOULD GIVE ME FOUR MINUTES,"

He stood and looked at me first in astonishment, afterward in pity. Finally tears welled up in his eyes, and plowed their way down his brown and grimy face. Then he said that I need not fear him. "You are safe," said he. "A youth who is so patient and so cheerful as you are—who would wait for a healthy man to die so that you could meander over his pulseless remnants, ought not to die a violent death. A soft-eyed seraph like you, who is no more conversant with the ways of this world than that, ought to be put in a glass vial of alcohol and preserved. I came up here to kill you and throw you into the rain-water barrel, but now that I know what a patient disposition you have, I shudder to think of the crime I was about to commit."

JOAQUIN AND JUNIATA.

JOAQUIN MILLER has just published a new book called "The Shadows of Shasta." It is based on the Hiawatha, Blue Juniata romance, which the average poet seems competent to yank loose from the history of the sore-eyed savage at all times.

Whenever a dead-beat poet strikes bedrock and don't have shekels enough to buy a bowl of soup, he writes an inspired ode to the unfettered horse-thief of the west.

It is all right so far as we know. If the poet will wear out the smoke-tanned child of the forest writing poetry about him, and then if the child of the forest will rise up in his death struggle and mash the never-dying soul out of the white-livered poet, everything will be O.K., and we will pay the funeral expenses.

If it could be so arranged that the poet and the bright Alfarita bug-eater and the bilious wild-eyed bard of the backwoods could be shut up in a corral for six weeks together, with nothing to eat but each other, it would be a big thing for humanity. We said once that we wouldn't dictate to this administration, but let it flicker along alone. We just throw out the above as a suggestion, however, hoping that it will not be ignored.

SOME VAGUE THOUGHTS.

SPRING, gentle, touchful, tuneful, breezeful, soothful spring is here. It has not been here more than twenty minutes, and my arctics stand where I can reach them in case it should change its mind.

The bobolink sits on the basswood vines, and the thrush in the gooseberry tree is as melodious as a hired man. The robin is building his nest—or rather her nest, I should say, perhaps—in the boughs of the old willow that was last year busted by thunder—I beg your pardon—by lightning, I should say. The speckled calf dines teat-a-teat with his mother, and strawberries are like a baldheaded man's brow—they come high, but we can't get along without them.

I never was more tickled to meet gentle spring than I am now. It stirs up my drug-soaked remains, and warms the genial current of life considerably. I frolicked around in the grass this afternoon and filled my pockets full of 1000-legged worms, and other little mementoes of the season. The little hare-foot boy now comes forth and walks with a cautious tread at first, like a blind horse; but toward the golden autumn the backs of his feet will look like a warty toad, and there will be big cracks in them, and one toe will be wrapped up in part of a bed quilt, and he will show it with pride to crowded houses.

Last night I lay awake for several hours thinking about Mr. Sherrod and how long we had been separated, and I was wondering how many weary days would have to elapse before we would again look into each other's eyes and hold each other by the hand, when the loud and violent concussion of a revolver shot near West Main street and Cascade avenue rent the sable robe of night. I rose and lit the gas to see if I had been hit. Then I examined my pockets to see if I had been robbed of my led pencil and season pass. I found that I had not.

This morning I learned that a young doctor, who had been watching his own house from a distance during the evening, had discovered that, taking advantage of the husband's absence, a blonde dry goods clerk had called to see the crooked but lonely wife. The doctor waited until the young man had been in the house long enough to get pretty well acquainted, and then he went in himself to see that the youth was making himself perfectly comfortable.

There was a wild dash toward the window, made by a blonde man with his pantaloons in his hand, the spatter of a bullet in the wall over the young man's head and then all was still for a moment save the low sob of a woman with her head covered up by the bed clothes. Then the two men clinched and the doctor injected the barrel of a thirty-two self-cocker up the bridge of the young man's nose, knocked him under the wash stand, yanked him out by the hem of his garment and jarred him into the coal bucket, kicked him up on a corner bracket and then swept the quivering ruins into the street with a stub-broom. He then lit the chandelier and told his sobbing wife that she wasn't just the temperament for him and he was afraid that their paths might diverge. He didn't care much for company and society while she seemed to yearn for such things constantly. He came right out and admitted that he was of a nervous temperament and quick tempered. He loved her, but he had such an irritable, fiery disposition that he guessed he would have to excuse her; so he escorted her out to the gate and told her where the best hotel was, came in, drove out the cat, blew out the light and retired.

Some men seem almost like brutes in their treatment of their wives. They come home at some eccentric hour of the night, and because they have to sleep on the lounge, they get mad and try to shoot holes in the lambrequins, and look at their wives in a harsh, rude tone of voice. I tell you it's tough.

THE YOUMORIST.

Y ou are an youmorist, are you not?" queried a long-billed pelican address-
ing a thoughtful, mental athlete, on the Milwaukee & St. Paul road the other day.

"Yes, sir," said the sorrowful man, brushing away a tear. "I am an youmorist.
I am not very much so, but still I can see that I am drifting that way. And yet I was
once joyous and happy as you are. Only a few years ago, before I was exposed to
this malady, I was as blithe as a speckled yearling, and recked not of aught—nor
anything else, either. Now my whole life is blasted. I do not dare to eat pie or
preserves, and no one tells funny stories when I am near. They regard me as a
professional, and when I get in sight the 'scrub nine' close up and wait for me to
entertain the crowd and waddle around the ring."

"What do you mean by that?" murmured the purple-nosed interrogation
point.

"Mean? Why, I mean that whether I'm drawing a salary or not, I'm expected
to be the 'life of the party.' I don't want to be the life of the party. I want to let some
one else be the life of the party. I want to get up the reputation of being as cross
as a bear with a sore head. I want people to watch their children for fear I'll swallow them. I want to take my low-cut-evening-dress smile and put it in the bureau
drawer, and tell the world I've got a cancer in my stomach, and the heaves and
hypochondria, and a malignant case of leprosy."

"Do you mean to say that you do not feel facetious all the time, and that you
get weary of being an youmorist?"

"Yes, hungry interlocutor. Yes, low-browed student, yes. I am not always tickled. Did you ever have a large, angry, and abnormally protuberent boil somewhere on your person where it seemed to be in the way? Did you ever have such a
boil as a traveling companion, and then get introduced to people as an youmorist?
You have not? Well, then, you do not know all there is of suffering in this sor-
row-streaked world. When wealthy people die why don't they endow a cast-iron
castle with a draw-bridge to it and call it the youmorists' retreat? Why don't they
do some good with their money instead of fooling it away on those who are comparatively happy?"

"But how did you come to git to be an youmorist?"

"Well, I don't know. I blame my parents some. They might have prevented it if
they'd taken it in time, but they didn't. They let it run on till it got established, and

now its no use to go to the Hot Springs or to the mountains, or have an operation performed. You let a man get the name of being an youmorist and he doesn't dare to register at the hotels, and he has to travel anonymously, and mark his clothes with his wife's name, or the public will lynch him if he doesn't say something youmorous.

"Where is your boy to-night?" continued the gloomy humorist. "Do you know where he is? Is he at home under your watchful eye, or is he away somewhere nailing the handles on his first little joke? Parent, beware. Teach your boy to beware. Watch him night and day, or all at once, when he is beyond your jurisdiction, he will grow pale. He will have a far-away look in his eye, and the bright, rosy lad will have become the flatchested, joyless youmorist.

"It's hard to speak unkindly of our parents, but mingled with my own remorse I shall always murmur to myself, and ask over and over, why did not my parents rescue me while they could? Why did they allow my chubby little feet to waddle down to the dangerous ground on which the sad-eyed youmorist must forever stand?

"Partner, do not forget what I have said to-day. 'Whether your child be a son or daughter, it matters not. Discourage the first sign of approaching humor. It is easier to bust the backbone of the first little, tender jokelet that sticks its head through the virgin soil, than it is to allow the slimy folds of your son's youmorous lecture to be wrapped about you, and to bring your gray hairs with sorrow to the grave."

MY CABINET.

I HAVE made a small collection of wild, western things during the past seven years, and have put them together, hoping some day, when I get feeble, to travel with the aggregation and erect a large monument of kopecks for my executors, administrators and assigns forever.

Beginning with the skull of old Hi-lo-Jack-and-the-game, a Sioux brave, the collection takes in my wonderful bird, known as the Walk-up-the-creek, and another *vara avis*, with carnivorous bill and web feet, which has astonished everyone except the taxidermist and myself. An old grizzly bear hunter—who has plowed corn all his life and don't know a coyote from a Maverick steer—looked at it last fall and pronounced it a "kingfisher," said he had killed one like it a year ago. Then I knew that he was a pilgrim and a stranger, and that he had bought his buckskin coat and bead-trimmed moccasins at Niagara Falls, for the bird is constructed of an eagle's head, a canvas back duck's bust and feet, with the balance sage hen and baled hay.

Last fall I desired to add to my rare collection a large hornet's nest. I had an embalmed tarantula and her porcelain-lined nest, and I desired to add to these the gray and airy home of the hornet. I procured one of the large size after cold weather and hung it in my cabinet by a string. I forgot about it until this spring. When warm weather came, something reminded me of it. I think it was a hornet. He jogged my memory in some way and called my attention to it. Memory is not located where I thought it was. It seemed as though whenever he touched me he awakened a memory—a warm memory with a red place all around it.

Then some more hornets came and began to rake up old personalities. I remember that one of them lit on my upper lip. He thought it was a rosebud. When he went away it looked like a gladiola bulb. I wrapped a wet sheet around it to take out the warmth and reduce the swelling so that I could go through the folding doors and tell my wife about it.

Hornets lit ah over me and walked around on my person. I did not dare to scrape them off because they are so sensitive. You have to be very guarded in your conduct toward a hornet.

I remember once while I was watching the busy little hornet gathering honey and June bugs from the bosom of a rose, years ago, I stirred him up with a club, more as a practical joke than anything else, and he came and lit in my sunny hair—that was when I wore my own hair and he walked around through my gleaming tresses quite awhile, making tracks as large as a watermelon all over my head. If he hadn't run out of tracks my head would have looked like a load of summer squashes. I remember I had to thump my head against the smoke-house in order to smash him, and I had to comb him out with a fine comb, and wear a waste-paper basket two weeks for a hat.

Much has been said of the hornet, but he has an odd, quaint way after all, that is forever new.

HEALTH FOOD.

WHILE trying to reconstruct a telescoped spine and put some new copper rivets in the lumbar vertebrae, this spring, I have had occasion to thoroughly investigate the subject of so-called health food, such as gruels, beef tea inundations, toasts, oat meal mush, bran mash, soups, condition powders, graham gem, ground feed, pepsin, laudable mush, and other hen feed usually poked into the invalid who is too weak to defend himself.

Of course it stands to reason that the reluctant and fluttering spirit may not be won back to earth, and joy once more beam in the leaden eye unless due care be taken relative to the food by means of which nature may be made to assert herself.

I do not care to say to the world through the columns of the Free Press, that we may woo from eternity the trembling life with pie. Welsh rabbit and other wild game will not do at first. But I think I am speaking the sentiments of a large and emaciated constituency when I say, that there is getting to be a strong feeling against oat meal submerged in milk and in favor of strawberry short cake.

I almost ate myself into an early grave in April by flying into the face of Providence and demoralizing old Gastric with oat meal. I ate oat meal two weeks, and at the end of that time my friends were telegraphed for, but before it was too late, I threw off the shackles that bound me. With a desperation born of a terrible apprehension, I rose and shook off the fatal oat meal habit and began to eat beefsteak. At first life hung trembling in the balance and there was no change in the quotations of beef, but later on there was a slight, delicate bloom on the wan cheek, and range cattle that had barely escaped a long, severe winter on the plains, began to apprehend a new danger and to seek the secluded canyons of the inaccessible mountains.

I often thought while I was eating health food and waiting for death, how the doctor and other invited guests at the post mortem would start back in amazement to find the remnants of an eminent man filled with bran!

Through all the painful hours of the long, long night and the eventless day, while the mad throng rushed onward like a great river toward eternity's ocean, this thought was uppermost in my mind. I tried to get the physician to promise that he would not expose me, and show the world what a hollow mockery I had been, and how I had deceived my best friends. I told him the whole truth, and asked him to spare my family the humiliation of knowing that though I might have led a blameless life, my sunny exterior was only a thin covering for bran and shorts and middlings, cracked wheat and pearl barley.

I dreamed last night of being in a large city where the streets were paved with dry toast, and the buildings were roofed with toast, and the soil was bran and oat meal, and the water was beef tea and gruel. All at once it came over me that I had solved the great mystery of death, and had been consigned to a place of eternal punishment. The thought was horrible! A million eternities in a city built of dry toast and oat meal! A home for never-ending cycles of ages, where the principal hotel and the post-office building and the opera house were all built of toast, and the fire department squirted gruel at the devouring element forever!

It was only a dream, but it has made me more thoughtful, and people notice that I am not so giddy as I was.

A NEW POET.

A NEW and dazzling literary star has risen above the horizon, and is just about to shoot athwart the starry vault of poesy. How wisely are all things ordered, and how promptly does the new star begin to beam, upon the decline of the old.

Hardly had the sweet singer of Michigan commenced to wane and to flicker, when, rising above the western hills, the glad light of the rising star is seen, and adown the canyons and gulches of the Rocky mountains comes the melodious cadences of the poet of the Greeley Eye.

Couched in the rough terms of the west; robed in the untutored language of the Michael Angelo slang of the miner and the cowboy, the poet at first twitters a little on a bough far up the canyon, gradually waking the echoes, until the song is taken up and handed back by every rock and crag along the rugged ramparts of the mighty mountain barrier.

Listen to the opening stanza of "The Dying Cowboy and the Preacher:"

> ``So, old gospel shark, they tell me I must die;
> ``That the wheels of life's wagon have rolled into their last rut,
> ``Well, I will "pass in my checks" without a whimper or a cry,
> ``And die as I have lived—"a hard nut."

This is no time-worn simile, no hackneyed illustration or bald-headed decrepit comparison, but a new, fresh illustration that appeals to the western character, and lifts the very soul out of the kinks, as it were.

"Wheels of life's wagon have rolled into their last rut."

Ah! how true to nature and yet how grand. How broad and sweeping. How melodious and yet how real. Hone but the true poet would have thought to compare the close of life to the sudden and unfortunate chuck of the off hind wheel of a lumber wagon into a rut.

In fancy we can see it all. We hear the low, sad kerplunk of the wheel, the loud burst of earnest, logical profanity, and then all is still.

How and then the swish of a mule's tail through the air, or the sigh of the rawhide as it shimmers and hurtles through the silent air, and then a calm falls upon the scene. Anon, the driver bangs the mule that is ostensibly pulling his daylights out, but who is, in fact, humping up like an angle worm, without pulling a pound.

Then the poet comes to the close of the cowboy's career in this style:

``Do I repent?" No—of nothing present or past;

So skip, old preach, on gospel pap I won't be fed;

My breath comes hard; I—am going—but—I—am game to the—last.

And reckless of the future, as the present, the cowboy was dead.=

If we could write poetry like that, do you think we would plod along the dreary pathway of the journalist? Do you suppose that if we had the heaven-born gift of song to such a degree that we could take hold of the hearts of millions and warble two or three little ditties like that, or write an effigy before breakfast, or construct an ionic, anapestic twitter like the foregoing, that we would carry in our own coal, and trim our own lamps, and wear a shirt two weeks at a time?

No, sir, he would hie us away to Europe or Salt Lake, and let our hair grow long, and we would write some obituary truck that would make people disgusted with life, and they would sigh for death that they might leave their insurance and their obituaries to their survivors.

A WORD IN SELF-DEFENSE.

IT might be well in closing to say a word in defense of myself.

The varied and uniformly erroneous notions expressed recently as to my plans for the future, naturally call for some kind of an expression on this point over my own signature. In the first place, it devolves upon me to regain my health in full if it takes fourteen years. I shall not, therefore, "publish a book," "prepare an youmorous lecture," "visit Florida," "probate the estate of Lydia E. Pinkham, deceased," nor make any other grand break till I have once more the old vigor and elasticity, and gurgling laugh of other days.

In the meantime, let it be remembered that my home is in Laramie City, and that unless the common council pass an ordinance against it, I shall return in July if I can make the trip between snow storms, and evade the peculiarities of a tardy and reluctant spring.

Bill Nye.

PINES FOE HIS OLD HOME.

TOM FAGAN, of this city, has a wild horse that don't seem to take to the rush and hurry and turmoil of a metropolis. He has been so accustomed to the glad, free air of the plains and mountains that the hampered and false life of a throbbing city, with its myriad industries, makes him nervous and unhappy. He sighs for the boundless prairie and the pure breath of the lifegiving mountain atmosphere. So taciturn is he in fact, and so cursed by homesickness and weariness of an artificial and unnatural horse society here in Laramie, that he refuses to eat anything and is gradually pining away. Sometimes he takes a light lunch out of Mr. Fagan's arm, but for days and days he utterly loathes food. He also loathes those who try to go into the stable and fondle him. He isn't apparently very much on the fondle. He don't yearn for human society, but seems to want to be by himself and think it over.

The wild horse in stories soon learns to love his master and stay by him and carry him through flood or fire, and generally knows more than the Cyclopedia Brittanica; but this horse is not the historical horse that they put into wild Arabian falsehoods. He is just a plain, unassuming wild horse of Wyoming descent, whose pedigree is slightly clouded, and who is sensitive on the question of his ancestry. All he wants is just to be let alone, and most everybody has decided that he is right. They came do that conclusion after they had soaked their persons in arnica and glued themselves together with poultices.

Perhaps, after a while, he will conclude to eat hay and grow up with the country, but now he sighs for his native bunch-grass and the buffalo wallow wherein he has heretofore made his lair. We don't wonder much, though, that a horse who has lived in the country should be a little rattled here when he finds the electric light, and bicycles, and lawn mowers, and Uncle Tom's Cabin troupes, and baled hay at $20 per ton. It makes him as wild and skittish as it does an eighteen-year-old girl the first time she comes into town, and for the first time is met by the blare of trumpets, and the oriental wealth of the circus with its deformed camels and uniformed tramps driving its miles of cages with no animals in them. The great natural world and the giddy maelstrom of seething, perspiring humanity, peculiar to the city world, are two separate and distinct existences.

"HE PINES FOR HIS OLD HOME,"

"He sighs for the boundless prairie."

ONE TOUCH OF NATURE.

U P in Polk county, Wisconsin, not long ago, a man who had lost eight children by diphtheria, while the ninth hovered between life and death with the same disease, went to the-health officer of the town and asked aid to prevent the spread of the terrible scourge. The health officer was cool and collected. He did not get excited over the anguish of the father whose last child was at that moment hovering upon the outskirts of immortality. He calmly investigated the matter, and never for a moment lost sight of the fact that he was a town officer and a professed Christian.

"You ask aid, I understand," said he, "to prevent the spread of the disease, and also that the town shall assist you in procuring new and necessary clothing to replace that which you have been compelled to burn in order to stop the further inroads of diphtheria. Am I right?" The poor man answered affirmatively.

"May I ask if your boys who died were Christian boys, and whether they improved their gospel opportunities and attended the Sabbath school, or whether they were profane and given over to Sabbath-breaking?"

The bereft father said that his boys had never made a profession of Christianity; that they were hardly old enough to do so, and that they might have missed some gospel opportunities owing to the fact that they were poor, and hadn't clothes fit to wear to Sabbath school. Possibly, too, they had met with wicked companions, and had been taught to swear; he could not say but they might have sworn, although he thought they would have turned out to be good boys had they lived.

"I am sorry that the case is so bad," said the health officer. "I am led to believe that God has seen fit to visit you with affliction in order to express His Divine disapproval of profanity, and I cannot help you. It ill becomes us poor, weak worms of the dust to meddle with the just judgments of God. Whether as an individual or as a *quasi corporation*, it is well to allow the Almighty to work out His great plan of salvation, and to avoid all carnal interference with the works of God."

The old man went back to his desolated home and to the bedside of his only living child. I met him yesterday and he told me all about it.

"I am not a professor of religion," said he, "but I tell you, Mr. Nye, I can't believe that this board of health has used me right. Somehow I ain't worried about my little fellers that is gone.

"They was little fellers, anyway, and they wasn't posted on the plan of salvation, but they was always kind and they always minded me and their mother. If God is using diphtheria agin perfanity this season they didn't know it. They was too young to know about it and I was too poor to take the papers, so I didn't know it nuther. I just thought that Christ was partial to kids like mine, just the same as He used to be 2,000 years ago when the country was new. I admit that my little shavers never went to Sabbath school much, and I wasn't scholar enough to throw much light onto God's system of retribution, but I told 'em to behave themselves, and they did, and we had a good deal of fun together—me and the boys—and they was so bright, and square, and cute that I didn't see how they could fall under divine wrath, and I don't believe they did.

"I could tell you lots of smart little things that they used to do, Mr. Nye, but they wa'n't mean and cussed. They was just frolicky and gay sometimes because they felt good. I don't believe God had it in for 'em bekuz they was like other boys, do you? Fer if I thought so it would kind o' harden me and the old lady and make us sour on all creation.

"Mind you, I don't kick because I'm left alone here in the woods, and the sun don't seem to shine, and the birds seems a little backward about singin' this spring, and the house is so quiet, and she is still all the time and cries in the night when she thinks I am asleep. All that is tough, Mr. Nye—tough as old Harry, too—but its so, and I ain't murmurin', but when the board of health says to me that the Ruler of the Universe is makin' a tower of Northern Wisconsin, mowin' down little boys with sore throat because they say 'gosh,' I can't believe it.

"I know that people who ain't familiar with the facts will shake their heads and say that I am a child of wrath, but I can't help it, All I can do is to go up there under the trees where them little graves is, and think how all-fired pleasant to me them little, short lives was, and how every one of them little fellers was welcome when he come, poor as I was, and how I rastled with poor crops and pine stumps to buy cloze for 'em, and didn't care a cent for style as long as they was well. That's the kind of heretic I am, and if God is like a father that settles it, He wouldn't wipe out my family just to establish discipline, I don't believe. The plan of creation must be on a bigger scale than that, it seems to me, or else it's more or less of a fizzle.

"That board of health is better read than I am. It takes the papers and can add up figures, and do lots of things that I can't do; but when them fellers tell me that they represent the town of Balsam Lake and the Kingdom of Heaven, my morbid curiosity is aroused, and I want to see the stiffykits of election."

HOW TO PUT UP A STOVE-PIPE.

PUTTING up stove-pipe is easy enough, if you only go at it right. In the morning, breakfast on some light, nutritious diet, and drink two cups of hot coffee; after which put on a suit of old clothes—or new ones, if you can get them on time—put on an old pair of buckskin gloves, and, when everything is ripe for the fatal blow, go and get a good hardware man who understands his business. If this rule be strictly adhered to, the gorgeous eighteen-karat-stem-winding profanity of the present day may be very largely diminished, and the world made better.

FUN OF BEING A PUBLISHER.

BEING a publisher is not all sunshine, joy and johnny-jump-ups, although the gentle and tractable reader may at times think so.

A letter was received two years ago by the publishers of this book, on the outside of which was the request to the "P. Master of Chicago to give to the most reliable man in Chicago and oblige."

The P. Master thereupon gave the letter to Messrs. Belford, Clarke & Co., who have sent it to me as a literary curiosity. I want it to go down to posterity, so I put it in this great work. I simply change the names, and where words are too obscure, doctor them up a little:

Butler, Bates county, Mo., Jan. the 2, 1881.

I have a novle fresh and pure from the pen, wich I would like to be examined by you. I wish to bring it before the public the ensuing summer.

I have wrote a good deal for the press, and always with great success. I wrote once an article on the growth of pie plant wich was copied fur and wide. You may have heard of me through my poem on "The Cold, Damp Sea or the Murmuring Wave and its Sad Kerplunk."

I dashed it off one summer day for the Scabtown *Herald*.

In it, I enter the fair field of fancy and with exquisite word-painting, I lead the reader on and on till he forgets that breakfast is ready, and follows the thrilling career of Algonquin and his own fair-haired Sciataca through page after page of delirious joy and poetic rithum.

In this novle, I have wove a woof of possibilities, criss-crossed with pictures of my own wild, unfettered fancy, which makes it a work at once truthful and yet sufficiently unnatural to make it egorly sot for by the great reading world.

The plot of the novle is this:

Algonquin is a poor artist, who paints lovely sunsets and things, nights, and cuts cordwood during the day, struggling to win a competence so that he can sue for the hand of Sciataca, the wealthy daughter of a plumber.

She does not love him much, and treats him coldly; but he perseveres till one of his exquisite pictures is egorly snapt up by a wealthy man at $2. The man afterwards turns out to be Sciataca's pa.

He says unkind things of Algonquin, and intimates that he is a better artist in four-foot wood than he is as a sunset man. He says that Algonquin is more of a Michael Angelo in basswood than anywhere else, and puts a wet blanket on Sciataca's love for Algonquin.

Then Sciataca grows colder than ever to Algonquin, and engages herself to a wealthy journalist.

Just as the wedding is about to take place, Algonquin finds that he is by birth an Ohio man. Sciataca repents and marries her first love. He secures the appointment of governor of Wyoming, and they remove to Cheyenne.

Then there are many little bursts of pictureskness and other things that I would like to see in print.

I send also a picture of myself which I would like to have in the book. Tell the artist to tone down the freckles so that the features may be seen by the observer, and put on a diamond pin, so that it will have the appearance of wealth, which the author of a book generally wears.

It is not wrote very good, but that won't make any difference when it is in print.

When the reading public begins to devour it, and the scads come rolling in, you can deduct enough for to pay your expenses of printing and pressing, and send me the balance by post-office money order. Please get it on the market as soon as possible, as I need a Swiss muzzlin and some other togs suitable to my position in liturary circles. Yours truly, Luella Blinker.

LINGERIE.

A LADY'S underwear is politely spoken of as "lingerie," but the great horrid man crawls into his decrepit last year's undershirt every Monday morning, and swears because his new underclothes are so "lingerie" about making their appearance.

FRUIT.

A CLASS of croakers that one meets with everywhere, have steadily maintained that fruit cannot be raised in this Territory. In conversation with a small boy yesterday, we learned that this is not true. It is very simple and easy to do, even in this rigorous climate. He showed us how it is done. He has a small and delicately constructed harpoon with a tail to it—the apparatus attached to a long string. He goes into the nearest market, and while the clerk is cutting out some choice steaks for the man with the store teeth, the boy throws his harpoon and hauls in on the string. In this way he raises all kinds of fruit, not only for his own use, but he has some to sell.

He showed us some that he raised. It was as good as any of the fruit that we buy here, only that there was a little hole on one side, but that don't hurt the fruit for immediate use. He "puts some down," but don't can or dry any. He says that he applies his where he feels the worst. When he feels as though a Greening or a Bellflower would help him, he goes out and picks it. He showed us a string with a grappling hook attached, on which he had raised a bushel of assorted fruit this fall, and it wasn't a very good string, either.

THE BONE OF CONTENTION.

TWO self-accused humorists of Ohio have had a fight over the authorship of the facetious phenomenon and laugh-jerking success, "Who ever saw a tree box?" The bone of contention between these two gigantic minds, evidently, is not their funny-bone.

CONGRATULATORY.

I CANNOT close this letter without writing my congratulations to Mr. Raymond, of *Tribune*, upon the position of Notary Public, which he has secured. True merit cannot long go unrewarded. I, too, am a Notary Public. So is Patterson of the Georgetown *Miner*. And yet we were all once poor boys, unknown and unrecognized. Patterson was the son of a wealthy editor in Michigan, who wished "Sniktau" to be a minister of the everlasting gospel, but "Snik." knew that he was destined to enter upon a wider and more important field. He devoted himself to the study of profanity in all its various branches, until now he can swear more men, and do a bigger "so-help-me-God" business than any other go-as-you-please affidavit man in Colorado.

I have held my office through a part of the administration of Grant, and all of the Hayes administration, so far, and all through the countless political changes of the territorial administration. I state this with a pardonable pride. It shows it was not the result of political influence or party, but was the natural outgrowth of official rectitude and just dealing toward all. When a man comes before me to make affidavit or to acknowledge a deed, I recognize no party, no friend. They are all served alike and charged alike.

I was appointed to this high official position under the administration of Governor Thayer. At that time C. O. D. French was secretary. I had to lubricate the wheels of government before I could catch on, as it were. C. O. D. French wanted $5. I sent it to him. I wrote him that when the people seemed determined to foist upon me the high official honor of Notary Public, the paltry sum of $5 should not stand in the way. I have held the position ever since. Political enemies have endeavored to tear to pieces my record, both officially and socially, but through evil and good report, I have still held it.

The nation to-day looks to her notaries public for her crowning glory and successful future. In their hands rest the might and the grandeur and the glory which, like a halo, in the years to come, will encircle the brow of Columbia. I feel the responsibility that rests upon me, and I tremble with the mighty weight of weal or woe for a great nation which hangs upon my every official act. I presume Mr. Raymond feels the same way. He ought, certainly, for the eyes of a great republic watch us with feverish anxiety. It is an awful position to be placed in. Let those who tread the lower walks of life envy not the brain-and-nerve-destroying position of the notary public, whose every movement is portentous, and great with its burden of good or ill for nations unborn. That is what is making an old man of me before my time, and sprinkling my strawberry blonde hair with gray.

THE AGONY IS OVER.

IT has occurred to us that the destruction of timber near the Continental Divide, in Colorado, which is also called, "The Backbone of the Continent," will naturally be a severe blow to the lumber region of Colorado.

We began studying on this joke last summer, and have wrestled prayerfully with it ever since, with the above result. Do not think, O gay, lighthearted reader, that these jokes are spontaneous, and that mirth is pumped out of the recesses of the editor's brain as a grocer pumps coal oil out of a tin tank. They come with fasting and sadness, and vexation of spirit, and groanings that cannot be uttered, and weeping and gnashing of teeth. Now that we are over this joke safely, no doubt that we shall begin to flesh up again.

OSTRICH CAVALRY.

THE question of mounting the United States cavalry upon ostriches, as a matter of economy, is being agitated on the strength of their easy propagation in Arizona and New Mexico. There being now one hundred and seventeen of these birds in that region, the result of the increase from nine of them imported several years ago. However successful ostrich farming may be in and of itself, we cannot speak too highly of the feasibility of using the bird for cavalry purposes. It is an established fact that the ostrich is very swift and will live for days without food, and be verier viceable all the time.

A detachment of ostrich cavalry could light out across the enemy's country like the wind, and easily distance an equal force mounted upon horses, and after several days' march, instead of a weary, worn, and jaded-out lot of horses, there would be a flock of ostriches, hungry but in good spirits, and the quartermasters could issue some empty bottles, and some sardine boxes, and some government socks, and an old blue overcoat or two, and the irons from an old ambulance, to each bird; and at evening, while the white tents were glimmering in the twilight, the birds would lie in a little knot chewing their cud constantly, and snoring in a subdued way that would shake the earth for miles around.

One great difficulty would be to keep a sufficient guard around the arms and ammunition to prevent the cavalry from eating them up. Think of a half dozen ostriches breaking into an inclosure while the guard was asleep, or off duty, and devouring fifteen or twenty rounds of ammunition in one night, or stealing into the place where the artillery was encamped, and filling themselves up with shells and round shot, and Greek fire and gatling guns.

AN ELECTRIC BELT.

A CHEYENNE man who was once mildly struck by lightning, calls it an "electric belt."

THE ANNUAL WAIL.

As usual, the regular fall wail of the eastern press on the Indian question, charging that the Indians never committed any depredations unless grossly abused, has arrived. We are unpacking it this morning and marking the price on it. Some of it is on manifold, and the remainder on ordinary telegraph paper. It will be closed out very cheap. Parties wishing to supply boarding schools with essays and compositions, cannot do better than to apply at once. We are selling Boston lots, with large brass-mounted words, at two and three cents per pound. Every package draws a prize of a two-pound can of baked beans. If large orders are received from any one person, we will set up the wail and start it to running, free of cost. It may be attached to any newspaper in a few minutes, and the merest child can readily understand it. It is very simple. But it is not as simple as the tallowy poultice on the average eastern paper, who grinds them out at $4 per week, and found.

We also have some old wails, two or three years old—and older—that have never been used, which we will sell very low. Old Sioux wails, Modoc wails, etc., etc. They do not seem to meet with a ready sale in the west, and we rather suspect it's because we are too near the scene of the Indian troubles. Parties who have been shot at, scalped, or had their wives and children massacred by the Indians, do not buy eastern wails.

Eastern wails are meant for the eastern market, and if we can get this old stock off our hands, we will hereafter treat the Indian question in our plain, matter of fact way.

The namby-pamby style of Indian editorial and molasses-candy-gush that New Englanders are now taking in, makes us tired. Life is too short. It is but a span. Only as a tale that has been told. Just like the coming of a guest, who gets his meal ticket punched, grabs a tooth pick, and skins out.

Then why do we fool away the golden years that the Creator has given us for mental improvement and spiritual elevation, in trying to fill up the enlightened masses with an inferior article of taffy?

Every man who knows enough to feed himself out of a maple trough, knows, or ought to know, that the Indian is treacherous, dishonest, diabolical and devilish in the extreme, and that he is only waiting the opportunity to spread out a little juvenile hell over the fair face of nature if you give him one-sixteenth of a chance. He will wear pants and comb his hair, and pray and be a class leader at the agency for fifty-nine years, if he knows that in the summer of the sixtieth year he can murder a few Colorado settlers and beat out the brains of the industrious farmers.

Industry is the foe of the red man. He is a warrior. He has royal blood in his veins, and the vermin of the Montezumas dance the German over his filthy carcass. That's the kind of a hair pin he is. He never works. Nobody but Chinamen and plebians ever work.

HE WAS NOT A BURGLAR.

THE young man who was seen climbing in a window on Center street yesterday, was not a burglar as some might suppose, but on the contrary he was a man whose wife had left the keys to the house lying on the mantel, and locked them in by means of a spring lock on the front door. He did not climb in the window because he preferred that way, but because the door unlocked better from the inside.

BEST ON, BLESSED MEMORY.

ONE of the attractions of life at the Cheyenne Indian agency, is the reserved seat ticket to the regular slaughter-house matinee. The agency butchers kill
at the rate of ten bullocks per hour while at work, and so great was the rush to the
slaughter-pens for the internal economy of the slaughtered animals, that Major
Love found it necessary to erect a box-office and gate, where none but those holding tickets could enter and provide themselves with these delicacies.

This is not a sensation, it is the plain truth, and we desire to call the attention of those who love and admire the Indian at a distance of 2,000 miles, and to
the aesthetic love for the beautiful which prompts the crooked-fanged and dusky
bride of old Fly-up-the-Creek to rob the soap-grease man and the glue factory, that
she may make a Cheyenne holiday. As a matter of fact, common decency will not
permit us to enter into a discussion of this matter. Firstly, it would not be fit for
the high order of readers who are now paying their money for *The Boomerang*; and
secondly, the Indian maiden at the present moment stands on a lofty crag of the
Rocky mountains, beautiful in her wild simplicity, wearing the fringed garments
of her tribe. To the sentimentalist she appears outlined against the glorious sky of
the new west, wearing a coronet of eagle's feathers, and a health-corset trimmed
with fantastic bead-work and wonderful and impossible designs in savage art.

Shall we then rush in and with ruthless hand shatter this beautiful picture?
Shall we portray her as she appears on her return from the great slaughter-house
benefit and moral aggregation of digestive mementoes? Shall we draw a picture
of her clothed in a horse-blanket, with a necklace of the false teeth of the pale
face, and her coarse unkempt hair hanging over her smoky features and clinging
to her warty, bony neck? No, no. Far be it from us to destroy the lovely vision of
copper-colored grace and smoke-tanned beauty, which the freckled student of the
effete east has erected in the rose-hued chambers of fancy. Let her dwell there as
the plump-limbed princess of a brave people. Let her adorn the hat-rack of his
imagination—proud, beautiful, grand, gloomy and peculiar—while as a matter of
fact she is at that moment leaving the vestibule of the slaughter-house, conveying
in the soiled lap-robe—which is her sole adornment—the mangled lungs of a Texas steer.

"REST ON, BLESSED MEMORY!"

Let the graceful Indian Queen live on.

No man shall ever say that we have busted the beautiful Cigar Sign Vision that he has erected in his memory. Let the graceful Indian queen that has lived on in his heart ever since he studied history and saw the graphic picture of the landing of Columbus, in which Columbus is just unsheathing his bread knife, and the stage Indians are fleeing to the tall brush; let her, we say, still live on. The ruthless hand that writes nothing but everlasting truth, and the stub pencil that yanks the cloak of the false and artificial from cold and perhaps unpalatable fact, null spare this little imaginary Indian maiden with a back-comb and gold garters. Let her withstand the onward march of centuries while the true Indian maiden eats the fricasseed locust of the plains and wears the cavalry pants of progress. We may be rough and thoughtless many times, but we cannot come forward and ruthlessly shatter the red goddess at whose shrine the far-away student of Black-hawk and other fourth-reader warriors, worship.

As we said, we decline to pull the cloak from the true Indian maiden of to-day and show her as she is. That cloak may be all she has on, and no gentleman will be rude even to the daughter of Old Bob-Tail-Flush, the Cheyenne brave.

A JUDICIAL WARBLER.

JACOB BEESON BLAIR, who has been recently renominated as associate justice of the Supreme Court of Wyoming, and judge of the second judicial district, with his headquarters at this place, is one of the most able and consistent officials that Wyoming ever had. I might go further and say that he stands at the head of them all. A year ago, as an evidence of his popularity, I will say that he was unanimously nominated to represent the Territory in Congress, which nomination he gracefully declined. He has put his spare capital into mines, and shown that he is a resident of Wyoming, and not of the classic halls of Washington, or the sea-beat shores of "Maryland, my Maryland."

Two years ago I had the pleasure of making a trip to the mines on Douglas creek, or, as it was then called, Last Chance, in company with Judge Blair and Delegate Downey, owners of the Keystone gold mine in that district. The party also included Governor Hoyt, Assayer Murphy, Postmaster Hayford, and several other prominent men. Judge Brown and Sheriff Boswell were also in the party at the mine. Judge Blair is, by natural choice, a Methodist, and renewed our spiritual strength throughout the trip in a way that was indeed pleasant and profitable. The Judge sings in a soft, subdued kind of a way that makes the walls of the firmament crack, and the heavens roll together like a scroll. When he sings —=

> How tedious and tasteless the hours
> When Jesus no longer I see,

the coyotes and jack-rabbits within a radius of seventy-five miles, hunt their respective holes, and remain there till the danger has passed.

Looking at the Judge as he sits on the bench singeing the road agent for ten years in solitary confinement, one would not think he could warble so when he gets into the mountains. But he can. He is a regular prima donna, so to speak.

When he starts to sing, the sound is like an Æolian harp, sighing through the pine forests and dying away upon the silent air. Gradually it swells into the wild melody of the hotel gong.

A FIRE AT A BALL.

OWN at Gunnison last week a large, select ball was given in a hall, one end of which was partitioned off for sleeping rooms. A young man who slept in one of these rooms, and who felt grieved because he had not been invited, and had to roll around and suffer while the glad throng tripped the light bombastic toe, at last discovered a knot-hole in the partition through which he could watch the giddy multitude. While peeping through the knot-hole, he discovered that one of the dancers, who had an aperture in the heel of his shoe and another in his sock to correspond, was standing by the wall with the ventilated foot near the knot-hole. It was but the work of a moment to hold a candle against this exposed heel until the thick epidermis had been heated red hot. Then there was a wail that rent the battlements above and drowned the blasts of the music. There was a wild scared cry of "fire": a frightened throng rushing hither and thither, and then, where mirth and music and rum had gladdened the eye and reddened the cheek a moment ago, all was still save the low convulsive titter of a scantily clad man, as he lay on the floor of his donjon tower and dug his nails in the floor.

A LITTLE PUFF.

SOME time ago the Cheyenne *Sun* noticed that Judge Crosby, known to Colorado and Wyoming people quite well, was making strenuous efforts, with some show of success, to obtain the appointment of Associate Justice of the Supreme Court of Wyoming. Since that, I have noticed with great sorrow that the President, in his youthful thoughtlessness and juvenile independence, has appointed another man for the position.

I speak of this because so many Colorado and Wyoming people knew Mr. Crosby and had an interest in him, as I might say. Some of us only knew him fifty cents worth, while others knew him for various amounts up to $5 and $10. He was an earnest, unflagging and industrious borrower. When times were dull he used to borrow of me. Then I would throw up my hands and let him go through me. It was not a hazardous act at all on my part.

The Judge knew everybody, and everybody knew him, and seemed nervous when they saw him, for fear that the regular assessment was about to be made. Every few days he wanted "to buy a pair of socks," but he never bought them. Forty or fifty of us got together and compared notes the other day. We ascertained that not less than $100 had been contributed to the Crosby Sock Fund during his stay here, and yet the old man wore the same socks to Washington that he had worn in the San Juan country. A like amount was also contributed to the Wash Bill Fund, and still he never had any washing done. We often wondered why so much money was squandered on laundry expenses, and yet, that he should have the general perspective and spicy fragrance of a Mormon emigrant train. He used to come into my office and be sociable with me because he was a journalist. It surprised me at first to meet a journalist who never changed his shirt. I thought that journalists, as a rule, wore diamond studs and had to be looked at through smoked glass.

He liked me. He told me so one day when we were alone, and after I had promised to tell no one. Then he asked me for a quarter. I told him I had nothing less than a fifty-cent piece. He said he would go and get it changed. I said it would be a shame for an old man, and lame at that, to go out and get it changed; so I said I would go. I went out and played thirteen of my eternal revolving games of billiards, and about dusk went back to the office whistling a merry roundelay, knowing that he had starved out and gone away. I found him at my desk, where he had written to every Senator and Representative in Congress, and every man who had ever been a Senator or Representative in Congress; likewise every man, woman and child who ever expected to be a Senator or a Representative in Congress; also, to every superintendent and passenger agent of every known line of railway, for a pass to every known point of the civilized world, and this correspondence he had used my letter heads, and envelopes and stamps, and he wasn't done either. He was just getting animated and warming up to his work, and perspiring so that I had to open the hall door and burn some old gum overshoes and other disinfectants before I could breathe.

A large society is being formed here and in Cheyenne, called the "Crosby Sufferer Aid Association." It is for the purpose of furnishing speedy relief to the sufferers from the Crosby outbreak. We desire the cooperation and assistance of Colorado philanthropists, and will, so far as possible, furnish relief to Colorado sufferers from the great scourge.

Later.—Henry Rothschild Crosby, Esq., passed through here a few evenings since, on his way to Evanston, Wyoming, where he takes charge of his office as receiver of public moneys for the western land office.

Henry seems to feel as though I had not stood by him through his political struggle at Washington. At least I learn from other parties that he does not seem to hunger and thirst after my genial society, and thinks that what little influence I may have had, has not been used in his interest.

That is where Henry hit the nail on the head, with that far-sighted statesmanship and clear, unerring logic for which he is so remarkable.

I do not blame those who were instrumental in securing his appointment, remember. Not at all. No doubt I would have done the same thing if I had been in Washington all winter, and Henry had hovered around me for breakfast, and for lunch, and for dinner, and for supper, and for between meals, and for picnics, and had borrowed my money, and my overcoat, and my meal ticket, and my bath ticket, and my pool checks, and my socks, and my *robs de nuit*, and my tooth brush, and my gas and writing materials and stationery; but it should be born in mind that I am a resident of Wyoming. I have property here and it behooves me to do and say what I can for the interests of our people. I may have to borrow some things myself some day and I don't want to find, then, that they have all been borrowed.

Let Hank stand back a little while and give the other boys a chance.

[Note.—In order to give the gentle reader an idea of Mr. Crosby's personal appearance, I have consented to draw a picture of him myself. It isn't very pretty, but it is horribly accurate. It is so life-like, that it seems as though I could almost detect his maroon-colored breath.—B. N]

CROSBY'S PORTRAIT, BY NYE.

GENIUS AND WHISKY.

I SEE in a recent issue of the *Sun* a short article clipped from a Sidney paper, relative to William Henry Harrison, which brings to my mind fresh recollections of the long ago. I knew William too. I knew him for a small amount which I wish I had now, to give to suffering Ireland. He came upon me in the prime of summer time and said he was a newspaper man. That always gets me. When a man says to me that he is a newspaper man, and proves it by showing the usual discouraging state of resources and liabilities, I always come forward with the collateral.

William wanted to go into the mountains and recover his exhausted nerve-force, and build up his brain-power with our dry, bracing air. He knew Mr. Foley, who was then working a claim in Last Chance, so he went out there to tone up his exhausted energies. He went out there, and after a few weeks a note came in from the man with the historical cognomen, asking me to send him a gallon of best Old Crow. I went to my guide book and encyclopoedia and ascertained that this was a kind of drink. I then purchased the amount and sent it on.

Mr. Foley said that William stayed by the jug till it was dry, and then he came into town. I met him on the street and asked him how his intellect seemed after his picnic in the mountains. He said she was all right now, and he felt just as though he could do the entire staff work on the New York *Herald* for two weeks and not sweat a hair. But he didn't pay for the Old Crow. It slipped his mind. When time hung heavy on my hands, I used to write William a note and cheerfully dun him for the amount. I would also ask him how his intellect seemed by this time, and also make other little jocular remarks. But he has never forwarded the amount. If the bill had been for pantaloons, or grub, or other luxuries, I might have excused him, but when I loan a man money for a staple like whisky. I don't think it's asking too much to hope that in the flight of time it would be paid back. However, I can't help it now. It's about time that another bogus journalist should put in an appearance. I have a few dollars ahead, and I am yearning to lay out the sum on struggling genius.

THE TWO-HEADED GIRL.

T HE cultivated two-headed girl has visited the west. It is very rare that a town the size of Laramie experiences the rare treat of witnessing anything so enjoyable. In addition to the mental feast which such a thing affords, one goes away feeling better—feeling that life has more in it to live for, and is not after all such a vale of tears as he had at times believed it.

Through the trials and disappointments of this earthly pilgrimage, the soul is at times cast down and discouraged. Man struggles against ill-fortune and unlooked-for woes, year after year, until he becomes misanthropical and soured, but when a two-headed girl comes along and he sees her it cheers him up. She speaks to his better nature in two different languages at one and the same time, and at one price.

When I went to the show I felt gloomy and apprehensive. The eighteenth ballot had been taken and the bulletins seemed to have a tiresome sameness. The future of the republic was not encouraging. I felt as though, if I could get first cost for the blasted thing, I would sell it.

I had also been breaking in a pair of new boots that day, and spectators had been betting wildly on the boots, while I had no backers at three o'clock in the afternoon, and had nearly decided to withdraw on the last ballot. I went to the entertainment feeling as though I should criticise it severely.

The two-headed girl is not beautiful. Neither one of her, in fact, is handsome. There is quite a similarity between the two, probably because they have been in each other's society a great deal and have adopted the same ways.

She is an Ethiopian by descent and natural choice, being about the same complexion as Frank Miller's oil blacking, price ten cents.

She was at one time a poor slave, but by her winning ways and genuine integrity and genius, she has won her way to the hearts of the American people. She has thoroughly demonstrated the fact that two heads are better than one.

A good sized audience welcomed this popular favorite. When she came forward to the footlights and made her two-ply bow she was greeted by round after round of applause from the *elite* of the city.

I felt pleased and gratified. The fact that a recent course of scientific lectures here was attended by from fifteen to thirty people, and the present brilliant success of the two-headed girl proved to me, beyond a doubt, that we live in an age of thought and philosophical progress.

Science may be all right in its place, but does it make the world better? Does it make a permanent improvement on the minds and thoughts of the listener? Do we go away from such a lecture feeling that we have made a grand stride toward a glad emancipation from the mental thraldom of ignorance and superstition? Do people want to be assailed, year after year, with a nebular theory, and the Professor Huxley theory of natural selections and things of that nature?

No! 1,000 times no!

They need to be led on quietly by an appeal to their better natures. They need to witness a first-class bureau of monstrosities, such as men with heads as big as a band wagon, women with two heads, Cardiff giants, men with limbs bristling out all over them like the velvety bloom on a prickly pear.

When I get a little leisure, and can attend to it,

I am going to organize a grand constellation of living wonders of this kind, and make thirteen or fourteen hundred farewell tours with it, not so much to make money, but to meet a long-felt, want of the American people for something which will give a higher mental tone to the tastes of those who never lag in their tireless march toward perfection.

THE CULTIVATION OF GUM.

AN idea has occurred to us, that, situated as we are at a considerable elevation, and being comparatively out of the line of tropical growth, we should try to propagate plants that will withstand the severe winter and the sudden and sometimes fatal surprise of spring. Plants in this locality worry along very well through the winter in a kind of semi-unconscious state, but when spring drops down on them about the Fourth of July they are not prepared for it, and they yield to the severe nervous shock and pass with a gentle gliding motion up the flume.

This has suggested to our mind the practicability of cultivating the chewing-gum plant. We advance this thought with some timidity, knowing that our enemies will use all these novel and untried ideas against us in a presidential campaign; but the good of the country is what we are after and we do not want to be misunderstood.

Chewing-gum is rapidly advancing in price, and the demand is far beyond the supply. The call for gum is co-extensive with the onward move of education. They may be said to go hand in hand. Wherever institutions of learning are found, there you will see the tall, graceful form of the chewing-gum tree rising toward heaven with its branches extending toward all humanity.

Here, in Wyoming, we could easily propagate this plant. It is hardy and don't seem to care whether winter lingers in the lap of spring or not. We have the figures, also, to substantiate this article. We will figure on the basis of twenty boxes of gum to the plant—and this is a very low estimate, indeed—then the plants may easily be three feet apart. This would be 3,097,600 plants to the acre, or 61,952,000 boxes, containing 100 chews in each box, or 6,195,200,000 chews to the acre. We have a million acres that could be used in this way, which would yield in a good year 6,195,200,000,000,000 chews at one cent each.

The reader will see at a glance that this is no wild romantic notion on our part, but a terrible reality. Wyoming could easily supply the present demand and wag the jaws of nations yet unborn. It makes us tired to think of it.

Of course, anything like this will meet with strong opposition on the part of those who have no faith in enterprises, but let a joint stock company be formed with sufficient capital to purchase the tools and gum seed, and we will be responsible for the result. Very likely the ordinary spruce gum (made of lard and resin) would be best as an experiment, after which the prize-package gum plant could be tried.

These experiments could be followed up with a trial of the gum drop, gum overshoe, gum arabic and other varieties of gum. Doctor Hayford would be a good man to take hold of this. Col. Donnellan says, however, that he don't think it is practical. No use of enlarging on this subject—it will never be tried. Probably the town is full of people who are willing to chew the gum, but wouldn't raise a hand toward starting a gum orchard. We are sick and tired of pointing out different avenues to wealth only to be laughed at and ridiculed.

WE HAVE REASONED IT OUT.

A HOME magazine comes to us this week, in which we find the following, connected with a society article. After alluding to the young men of the nineteenth century, and their peculiarities, it continues: "In fact, many of the more fashionable strains are all black, except the distinctive white feet and snout, so noticeable at this epoch in our history."

This, it would seem, will make a radical change in the prevailing young man. With white feet and white snout, the masher must also be black aside from those features. This will add the charm of extreme novelty to our social gatherings, and furnish sufficient excuse for a man like us, with blonde rind and strawberry blonde feet, staying at home, with the ban of society and a loose smoking jacket on him.

Farther on, this peculiar essay says: "He is noted for his wonderfully fine blood, the bone is fine, the hair thin, the carcass long but broad, straight and deep-sided, with smooth skin, susceptible to no mange or other skin diseases."

We almost busted our capacity trying to figure out this startler in the fashion line, and wore ourself down to a mere geometrical line in our endeavor to fathom this thing when, yesterday, in reading an article in the same paper entitled, "The Berkshire Hog," we discovered that the sentences above referred to had evidently been omitted by the foreman, and put in the society article. It is unnecessary to state that a blessed calm has settled down in the heart of this end of *The Boomerang*. Time, at last, makes all things size up in proper shape. Blessed be the time which matures the human mind and the promissory note.

CARVING SCHOOLS.

THEY are agitating the matter of instituting carving schools in the east, so that the rising generation will be able to pass down through the corridors of time without its lap full of dressing and its bosom laden with gravy and remorse. The students at this school will wear barbed-wire masks while practicing. These masks will be similar to those worn by German students, who slice each other up while obtaining an education.

DIGNITY.

COLONEL INGERSOLL said, at Omaha the other day, that he hated a dignified man and that he never knew one who had a particle of sense; that such men never learned, and were constantly forgetting something.

Josh Billings says that gravity is no more the sign of mental strength than a paper collar is the evidence of a shirt.

This leads us to say that the man who ranks as a dignified snoozer, and banks on winning wealth and a deathless name through this one source of strength, is in the most unenviable position of any one we know. Dignity does not draw. It answers in place of intellectual tone for twenty minutes, but after awhile it fails to get there. Dignity works all right in a wooden Indian or a drum major, but the man who desires to draw a salary through life and to be sure of a visible means of support, will do well to make some other provision than a haughty look and the air of patronage. Colonel Ingersoll may be wrong in the matter of future punishment, but his head is pretty level on the dignity question. Dignity works all right with a man who is worth a million dollars and has some doubts about his suspenders; but the man who is to get a large sum of money before he dies, and get married and accomplish some good, must place himself before his fellow men in the attitude of one who has ideas that are not too lonely and isolated.

Let us therefore aim higher than simply to appear cold and austere. Let us study to aid in the advancement of humanity and the increase of baled information. Let us struggle to advance and improve the world, even though in doing so we may get into ungraceful positions and at times look otherwise than pretty. Thus shall we get over the ground, and though we may do it in the eccentric style of the camel, we will get there, as we said before, and we will have camped and eaten our supper while the graceful and dignified pedestrian lingers along the trail.

Works, not good clothes and dignity, are the grand hailing sign, and he who halts and refuses to jump over an obstacle because he may not do it so as to appear as graceful as a gazelle, will not arrive until the festivities are over.

A SNORT OF AGONY.

OUR attention has been called to a remark made by the New York *Tribune*, which would intimate that the journal referred to didn't like Acting-Postmaster F. Hatton, and characterizing the editor of The Boomerang as a "journalistic pal" of General Hatton's. We certainly regret that circumstances have made it necessary for us to rebuke the *Tribune* and speak, harshly to it. Frank Hatton may be a journalistic pal of ours. Perhaps so. We would be glad to class him as a journalistic pal of ours, even though he may not have married rich. We think just as much of General Hatton as though he had married wealthy. We can't all marry rich and travel over the country, and edit our papers vicariously. That is something that can only happen to the blessed few.

It would be nice for us to go to Europe and have our *pro tem.* editor at home working for $20 per week, and telegraphing us every few minutes to know whether he should support Cornell or Folger. The pleasure of being an editor is greatly enhanced by such privileges, and we often feel that if we could get away from the hot, close office of The Boomerang, and roam around over Scandahoovia and the Bosphorus, and mould the policy of *The Boomerang* by telegraph, and wear a cork helmet and tight pants, we would be far happier. Still it may be that Whitelaw Reid is no happier with his high priced wife and his own record of crime, than we are in our simplicity here in the wild and rugged west, as we write little epics for our one-horse paper, and borrow tobacco of the foreman.

It is not all of life to live, nor all of death to die. We should live for a purpose, Mr. Reid, not aimlessly like a blind Indian, 200 miles from the reservation at Christmas-tide.

Now, Mr. Reid, if you will just tell Mr. Nicholson, when you get back home, that in referring to us as a journalistic pal of Frank Hatton he has exceeded his authority, we will feel grateful to you—and so will Mr. Hatton. If you don't do it, we shall be called upon to stop the *Tribune*, and subscribe for *Harper's Weekly*. This we should dislike to do very much, because we have taken the *Tribune* for years. We used to take it when the editor stayed at home and wrote for it. Our father used to take the *Tribune*, too. He is the editor of the Omaha *Republican*, and needs a good New York paper, but he has quit taking the *Tribune*. He said he must withdraw his patronage from a paper that is edited by a tourist. All the Nyes will now stop taking the *Tribune*, and all subscribe for some other dreary paper. We don't know just whether it will be *Harper's Weekly*, or the *Shroud*.

Later.—Mr. Reid went through here on Tuesday, and told us that he might have been wrong in referring to us as a journalistic pal of Frank Hatton, and in fact did not know that the *Tribune* had said so. He simply told Nicholson to kind of generally go for the administration, and turn over a great man every morning with his scathing pen, and probably Nicholson had kind of run out of great men, and tackled the North American Indian fighter of *The Boomerang*. Mr. Reid also said, as he rubbed some camphor ice on his nose, and borrowed a dollar from his wife to buy his supper here, that when he got back to New York, he was going to write some pieces for the *Tribune* himself. He was afraid he couldn't trust Nicholson, and the paper had now got where it needed an editor right by it all the time. He said also that he couldn't afford to be wakened up forty times a night to write telegrams to New York, telling the *Tribune* who to indorse for governor. It was a nuisance, he said, to stand at the center of a way station telegraph office, in his sun-flower night shirt, and write telegrams to Nicholson, telling him who to sass the next morning. Once, he said, he telegraphed him to dismember a journalistic pal of Frank Hatton's, and the operator made a mistake. So the next morning the *Tribune* had a regular old ring-tail peeler of an editorial, which planted one of Mr. Reid's special friends in an early grave. So we may know from this that moulding the course of a great paper by means of red messages, is fraught with some unpleasant features.

"A SNORT OF AGONY."

ALWAYS BOOM AT THE TOP.

Young man, do not stand lounging on the threshold of the glorious future, while the coming years are big with possibilities, but take off your coat and spit on your hands and win the wealth which the world will yield you. You may not be able to write a beautiful poem, and die of starvation; but you can go to work humbly as a porter and buy a whisk broom, and wear people's clothes out with it, and in five years you can go to Europe in your own special car. As the strawberry said to the box, "there is always room at the top."

INACCURATE.

ONCE more has Laramie been, slandered and traduced. Once more our free and peculiar style has been spoken lightly of and our pride trailed in the dust.

Last week the *Police Gazette*, an illustrated family journal of great merit, appeared with a half page steel engraving, executed by one of the old masters, representing two Laramie girls on horseback yanking a fly drummer along the street at a gallop, because he tried to make a mash on them and they did not yearn for his love.

There are two or three little errors in the illustration, to which we desire to call the attention of the eastern reader of Michael Angelo masterpieces that appear in the Police Gazette. First, the saloon or hurdy-gurdy shown in the left foreground is not the exact representation of any building in Laramie, and the dobe pig pens and A tents of which the town seems to be composed, are not true to nature.

Again, the streets do not look like the streets of Laramie. They look more like the public thoroughfares of Tie City or Jerusalem. Then the girls do not look like Laramie girls, and we are acquainted with all the girls in town, and consider ourself a judge of those matters. The girls in this illustration look too much as though they had mingled a great deal with the people of the world. They do not have that shy, frightened and pure look that they ought to have. They appear to be that kind of girls that one finds in the crowded metropolis under the gas light, yearning to get acquainted with some one.

There are several features of the illustration which we detect as erroneous, and among the rest we might mention, casually, that the incident illustrated never occurred here at all. Aside from these little irregularities above named, the picture is no doubt a correct one. We realize fully that times get dull even in New York sometimes, and it is necessary, occasionally, to draw on the imagination, but the *Gazette* artist ought to pick up some hard town like Cheyenne, and let us alone awhile.

THE WESTERN "CHAP."

Few know how voraciously we go for anything in the fashion line. Many of our exchanges are fashion magazines, and nothing is read with such avidity as these highly pictorial aggregations of literature. If there are going to be any changes in the male wardrobe this winter, it behooves us to know what they are. We intend to do so. It is our high prerogative and glorious privilege to live in a land of information. If we do not provide ourself with a few, it is our own fault. Man has spanned the ocean with an electric cable, and runs his street cars with another cable that puts people out of their misery as quick as a giant-powder caramel in a man's chest-protector, under certain circumstances. Science has done almost everything for us, except to pay our debts without leaning toward repudiation. We are making rapid strides in the line of progression. That is, the scientists are. Every little while you can hear a scientist burst a basting thread off his overalls, while making a stride.

It is equally true that we are marching rapidly along in the line of fashion. Change, unceasing change, is the war cry, and he who undertakes to go through the winter with the stage costumes of the previous winter, will find, as Voltaire once said, that it is a cold day.

We look with great concern upon the rapid changes which a few weeks have made. The full voluptuous swell and broad cincha of the chaparajo have given place to the tight pantaletts with feathers on them, conveying the idea that they cannot be removed until death, or an earthquake shall occur..

"Chaps," as they are vulgarly called, deserve more than a passing notice. They are made of leather with fronts of dog-skin with the hair on. The inside breadths are of calf or sheep-skin, made plain, but trimmed down the side seam with buckskin bugles and oil-tanned bric-a-brac of the time of Michael Angelo Kelley. On the front are plain pockets used for holding the ball programme and the "pop." The pop is a little design in nickel and steel, which is often used as an inhaler. It clears out the head, and leaves the nasal passages and phrenological chart out on the sidewalk, where pure air is abundant. "Chaps" are rather attractive while the wearer is on horseback, or walking toward you, but when he chasses and "all waltz to places," you discern that the seat of the garment has been postponed *sine die*. This, at first, induces a pang in the breast of the beholder. Later, however, you become accustomed to the barren and perhaps even stern demeanor of the wearer. You gradually gain control of yourself and master your raging desire to rush up and pin the garment together. The dance goes on. The *elite* take an adult's dose of ice-cream and other refreshments; the leader of the mad waltz glides down the hall with his mediæval "chaps," swishing along as he sails; the violin gives a last shriek; the superior fiddle rips the robe of night wide open, with a parting bzzzzt; the mad frolic is over, and $5 have gone into the dim and unfrequented freight depot of the frog-pond-environed past.

AN INCIDENT OF THE CAMPAIGN.

COLONEL THOMAS JUNIUS DAYTON entered the democratic headquarters on Second street, a few nights ago, having been largely engaged, previously, in talking over the political situation, with sugar in it. The first person he saw on entering, was an individual in the back part of the room, writing.

Colonel Dayton ordered him out.

The man would not go, maintaining that he had a right to meet together in democratic headquarters as often as he desired. The Colonel still insisted that he was an outsider and could have nothing in common with the patriotic band of bourbons whose stamping ground he had thus entered.

Finally the excitement became so great that a man was called in to umpire the game and sponge off the hostiles, but before blood was shed a peacemaker asked Colonel Dayton what the matter was with him.

"This man is a Democrat. I've known him for years. What's the reason you don't want him in here?"

"That's all right," said the Colonel, with his eyes starting from their sockets with indignation, "you people can be easily fooled. I cannot. I know him to be a spy in our camp. I have smelled his breath and find he is not up in the Ohio degree. I have also discovered him to be able to read and write. He cannot answer a single democratic test. He is a bogus bourbon, and my sentiments are that he should be gently but firmly fired. If the band will play something in D that is kind of tremulous, I will take off my coat and throw the gentleman over into a vacant lot. I think I know a Democrat when I see him. Perhaps you do not. He cannot respond to a single grand hailing sign. He hasn't the cancelled internal revenue stamp on his nose, and his breath lacks that spicy election odor which we know so well. Away with him! Fling his palpitating remains over the drawbridge and walk on him. Spread him out on the ramparts and jam him into the culverin. Those are my sentiments. We want no electroplate Democrats here. This is the stronghold of the highly aesthetic and excessively *bon-ton*, Andrew Jackson peeler, and if justice cannot be done to this usurper by the party, I shall have to go out and get an infirm hoe handle and administer about $9 worth of rebuke myself."

He went out after the hoe handle, and while absent, the stranger said he didn't want to be the cause of any ill feeling, or to stand in the way of the prosperity of his party, so he would not remain. He put on his hat and stole out into the night, a quiet martyr to the blind rage of Colonel Dayton, and has not since been seen.

WHY DO THEY DO IT?

BEN HILL, died, after suffering intolerable anguish from a tobacco cancer, caused by excessive smoking. The consumers of the western-made cigar are now and then getting a nice little dose of leprosy from the Chinese constructed cigars of San Francisco, and yet people go right on inviting the most horrible diseases known to science, by smoking, and smoking to excess. Why do they do it? It is one of those deep, dark mysteries that nothing but death can unravel. We cannot fathom it, that's certain. (Give us a light, please.)

TWO STYLES.

O NE of the peculiarities of correspondence is witnessed at this office every day, to which we desire to call the attention of our growing girls and boys, who ought to know that there is a long way and a short way of saying things on paper; a right way and a wrong way to express thoughts on a postal card, just as there is in conversation. We all admire the business man who is terse and to the point, and we dislike the man who hangs on to the door knob as though life was a never-ending summer dream, and refuses to say good-bye. It's so with correspondence. In touching upon the letters received at this office, we refer to a car load received at this office during the past year, relating to sample copies. Still they are a good specimen of the different styles of doing the same thing.

For instance, here is a line which tells the story in brief, without wearing out your eyes and days by ponderous phrases and useless verbiage. "Useless verbiage and frothy surplusage" is a synonym which we discovered in '75, while excavating for the purpose of laying the foundations of our imposing residence up the gulch. Persons using the same will please fork over ten per cent of the gross receipts:

"Bangor, Maine, 11-10-82.

"Find 10c for which send sample copy Boomerang to above address.

Yours, etc.,
"Thomas Billings."

Some would have said "please" find inclosed ten cents. That is not absolutely necessary. If you put ten cents in the letter that covers all seeming lack of politeness and it's all right. If, however, you are out of a job, and have nothing else to do but to write for sample copies of papers, and wait for the department at Washington to allow you a pension, you might say, "Please find inclosed," etc., otherwise the ten cents will make it all right.

Here's another style, which evinces a peculiarity we do not admire. It bespeaks the man who thinks that life and its associations are given us in order to wear out the time, waiting patiently meanwhile for Gabriel to render his little overture.

It occurs to us that life is real, life is earnest, and so forth. We cannot sit here in the gathering gloom and read four pages of a letter, which only expresses what ought to have been expressed in four lines. We feel that we are here to do the greatest good to the greatest-number, and we dislike the correspondent who hangs on to the literary door knob, so to speak, and absorbs our time, which is worth $5.35

per hour.

Here we go—

"New Centreville, Wis., Nov. 8, 1882.

"Mr. William Nye, esq., Laramie City, Wyoming:

"Dear Sir:—I have often saw in our home papers little pieces cut out of your paper The Larmy Boomerang, yet I have never saw the paper itself. I hardly pick up a paper, from the Fireside. Friend to the Christian at Work, that I do not see something or a nother from your faseshus pen and credited to *The Boomerang*. I have asked our bookstore for a copy of the paper, and he said go to grass, there wasn't no such perioddickle in existence. He is a liar; but I did not tell him so because I am just recovering from a case of that kind now, which swelled both eyes shet and placed me under the doctor's care.

"It was the result of a campaign lie, and at this moment I do not remember whether it was the other man or me which told it. Things got confused and I am not clear on the matter now.

"I send ten cents in postage stamps, hoping you will favor me with a speciment copy of *The Boomerang* and I may suscribe. I send postage stamps because they are more convenient to me, and I suppose that you can use them all right as you must have a good deal of writing to do. I intend to read the paper thorrow and give my folks the benefit also. I love to read humerrus pieces to my children and my wife and hear their gurgly laugh well up like a bobollink's. I now take an estern paper which is gloomy in its tendencies, and I call it the Morg. It looks at the dark side of life and costs $3 a year and postage.

"So send the speciment if you please and I will probbly suscribe for The Boomerang, as I have saw a good many extrax from it in our papers here and I have not as yet saw your paper."

GOSHALLHEMLOCK SALVE.

THE bullwacking, mule-skinning proprieter of a life-giving salve wants us to advertise for him, and to state that, with his Goshallhemlock salve he "can cure all chronicle diseases whatever."

"We would do it if we could, sweet being; but owing to the fullness of the paper and the foreman, we must turn you cruelly away.

"Yours truly,
"James Letson."

THE STAGE BALD-HEAD.

MOST everyone, who was not born blind, knows that the stage bald-head is a delusion and a snare. The only all-wool, yard-wide bald-head we remember on the American stage, is that of Dunstan Kirke as worn by the veteran Couldock.

Effie Ellsler wears her own hair and so does Couldock, but Couldock wears his the most. It is the most worn anyhow.

What we started out to say, is, that the stage bald-head and the average stage whiskers make us weary with life. The stage bald-head is generally made of the internal economy of a cow, dried so that it shines, and cut to fit the head as tightly as a potatoe sack would naturally fit a billiard cue. It is generally about four shades whiter than the red face of the wearer, or *vice versa*. We do not know which is the worst violation of eternal fitness, the red-faced man who wears a deathly white bald-head, or the pale young actor who wears a florid roof on his intellect. Sometimes in starring through the country and playing ten or fifteen hundred engagements, a bald-head gets soiled. We notice that when a show gets to Laramie the chances are that the bald-head of the leading old man is so soiled that he really needs a sheep-dip shampoo. Another feature of this accessory of the stage is its singular failure to fit. It is either a little short at both ends, or it hangs over the skull in large festoons, and wens and warts, in such a way as to make the audience believe that the wearer has dropsy of the brain.

You can never get a stage bald-head near enough like nature to fool the average house-fly. A fly knows in two moments whether it is the genuine, or only a base imitation, and the bald-head of the theatre fills him with nausea and disgust. Nature, at all times hard to imitate, preserves her bald head as she does her sunny skies and deep blue seas, far beyond the reach of the weak, fallible, human imitator. Baldness is like fame, it cannot be purchased. It must be acquired. Some men may be born bald, some may acquire baldness, and others may have baldness thrust upon them, but they generally acquire it.

"The stage beard is also rather dizzy, as a rule. It looks as much like a beard that grew there, as a cow's tail would if tied to the bronze dog on the front porch. When you tie a heavy black beard on a young actor, whose whole soul would be churned up if he smoked a full-fledged cigar, he looks about as savage as a bowl of mush and milk struck with a club."

FATHERLY WORDS.

N. W. P., writes:—"I am a young man twenty-five years old. I am in love with a young lady of seventeen. Her mind being very different from mine, I have not told her of my love, nor asked to call on her. I thought her so giddy that she did not want any steady company. She is a great lover of amusement. She is a perfect lady in her deportment, although she is more like a child of fourteen than a young lady of seventeen. I think she is very pretty, but she seems to enjoy flirting to the greatest extent. One evening at a party I asked her to promenade with me, and she would not do it. I then asked her to allow me to bring her refreshments, which she would not do. I then asked her to let me take her home when she was ready to go, and the answer was, 'No, I will not do any such thing,' and turning round she left me. I have met her several times since. She always bows to me. Everywhere she meets me she recognizes me pleasantly. How, did I do wrong in asking her those privileges at the party, I having no introduction to her? I am still in love with her."

After she had refused to promenade with you, and had declined to permit you to bring her refreshments, it was pressing matters rather too far for you to ask her to allow you to accompany her home "whenever she was ready to go." Still, as she treats you kindly whenever you meet, it is evident that you did not offend her very deeply. Perhaps she sees that you love her, and does not wish to discourage you.

You were, no doubt, a little previous in trying to get acquainted with the young lady. She may be giddy, but she has just about sized you up in shape, and no doubt, if you keep on trying to love her without her knowledge or consent, she will hit you with something, and put a Swiss sunset over your eye. Do not yearn to win her affections all at once. Give her twenty or thirty years in which to see your merits. You will have more to entitle you to her respect by that time, no doubt. During that time you may rise to be president and win a deathless name.

The main thing you have to look out for now, however, is to restrain yourself from marrying people who do not want to marry you. That style of freshness will, in thirty or forty years, wear away. If it does not, probably the vigorous big brother of some young lady of seventeen, will consign you to the silent tomb. Do not try to promenade with a young lady unless she gives her consent. Do not marry anyone against her wishes. Give the girl a chance. She will appreciate it, and even though she may not marry you, she will permit you to sit on the fence and watch her when she goes to marry some one else. Do not be despondent. Be courageous, and some day, perhaps, you will get there. At present the horizon is a little bit foggy.

As you say, she may be so giddy that she doesn't want steady company. There is a glimmer of hope in that. She may be waiting till she gets over the agony and annoyance of teething before she looks seriously into the matters of matrimony. If that should turn out to be the case we are not surprised. Give her a chance to grow up, and in the meantime, go and learn the organ grinder's profession and fix yourself so that you can provide for a family. Sometimes a girl only seventeen years old is able to discern that a young intellectual giant like you is not going to make a dazzling success of life as a husband. Brace up and try to forget your sorrow, N. W. P., and you may be happy yet.

THE GOOD TIME COMING.

ANGORA cloth is a Parisian novelty. Shaggy woolen goods are all the rage, and this Angora cloth is a perfect type of shaggy materials. It is a soft, downy article, like the fur of an Angora cat. Very showy toilets are of Angora cloth, trimmed with velvet applique work to form passementerie.

Angora cloth may be fashionable, but the odor of the Angora goat is losing favor. A herd of these goats crossed the Sierra Nevadas during the autumn, and as soon as they got over the range, we knew it at Laramie just as well as we knew of the earthquake shock on the 7th instant.

The Angora goat is very quiet in other respects; but as a fragrant shrub, he certainly demands attention. A little band of Angora goats has been quartered in Laramie City lately, and though they have been well behaved, they have made them have opened the casement to let in the glorious air of heaven. In letting in the glorious air of heaven, we have in several instances let in a good deal of the mohair industry and some seductive fragrance.

There is a glowing prospect that within the next year a bone fertilizer mill, a soap emporium and a glue factory will have been started here; and now, with the Angora goat looming up in the distance with his molasses-candy horns, his erect, but tremulous and undecided tail piercing the atmosphere, and the seductive odor peculiar to this fowl, we feel that life in Wyoming will not, after all, be a hollow mockery. Heretofore we have been compelled to worry along with polygamy and the odor of the alkali flat; but times are changing now, and we will one day have all the wonderful and complicated smells of Chicago at our door. Then will the desert indeed blossom as the rose, and the mountain lion and "Billy the Kid" will lie down together.

MANIA FOR MARKING CLOTHES.

THE most quiet, unobtrusive man I ever knew," said Buck Bramel to a Boomekang man, "was a young fellow who went into North Park in an early day from the Salmon river. He was also reserved and taciturn among the miners, and never made any suggestions if he could avoid it. He was also the most thoughtful man about other people's comfort I ever knew.

"I went into the cabin one day where he was lying on the bed, and told him I had decided to go into Laramie for a couple of weeks to do some trading. I put my valise down on the floor and was going out, when he asked me if my clothes were marked. I told him that I never marked my clothes. If the washerwoman wanted to mix up my wardrobe with that of a female seminary, I would have to stand it, I supposed.

"He thought I ought to mark my clothes before I went away, and said he would attend to it for me. So he took down his revolver and put three shots through the valise.

"After that a coolness sprang up between us, and the warm friendship that had existed so long was more or less busted. After that he marked a man's clothes over in Leadville in the same way, only the man had them on at the time. He seemed to have a mania on that subject, and as they had no insanity experts at Leadville in those days, they thought the most economical way to examine his brain would be to hang him, and then send the brain to New York in a baking powder can.

"So they hung him one night to the bough of a sighing mountain pine.

"The autopsy was, of course, crude; but they sawed open his head and scooped out the brain with a long handled spoon and sent it on to New York. By some mistake or other it got mixed up with some sample specimens of ore from 'The Brindle Tom Cat' discovery, and was sent to the assayer in New York instead of the insanity smelter and refiner, as was intended.

"The result was that the assayer wrote a very touching and grieved letter to the boys, saying that he was an old man anyway, and he wished they would consider his gray hairs and not try to palm off their old groceries on him. He might have made errors in his assays, perhaps—all men were more or less liable to mistakes— but he flattered himself that he could still distinguish between a piece of blossom rock and a can of decomposed lobster salad, even if it was in a baking-powder can. He hoped they would not try to be facetious at his expense any more, but use him as they would like to be treated themselves when they got old and began to totter down toward the silent tomb.

MANIA FOR MARKING CLOTHES.

Novel way of marking clothes.

"This is why we never knew to a dead moral certainty, whether he was O. K. in the upper story, or not."

REGARDING THE NOSE.

THE annals of surgery contain many cases where the nose has been cut or torn off, and being replaced has grown fast again, recovering its jeopardized functions. One of the earliest, 1680, is related by the surgeon (Fioraventi) who happened to be near by when a man's nose, having been cut off, had fallen in the sand. He remarks that he took it up, washed it, replaced it, and that it grew together.

Still, this is a little bit hazardous, and in warm weather the nose might refuse to catch on. It would be mortifying in the extreme to have the nose drop off in a dish of ice-cream at a large banquet. Not only would it be disagreeable to the owner of the nose, but to those who sat near him.

He adds the address of the owner of the repaired nose, and requests any doubter to go and examine for himself. Régnault, in the *Gazette Salutaire*, 1714, tells of a patient whose nose was bitten off by a smuggler. The owner of the nose wrapped it in a bit of cloth and sought Régnault, who, "although the part was cold, reset it, and it became attached."

This is another instance where, by being sufficiently previous, the nose was secured and handed down to future generations. Yet, as we said before, it is a little bit risky, and a nose of that character cannot be relied upon at all times. After a nose has once seceded it cannot be expected to still adhere to the old constitution with such loyalty as prior to that change.

Although these cases call for more credulity than most of us have to spare, yet later cases, published in trustworthy journals, would seem to corroborate this. In the *Clinical Annals* and *Medical Gazette*, of Heidelberg, 1830, there are sixteen similar cases cited by the surgeon (Dr. Hofacker) who was appointed by the senate to attend the duels of the students.

It seems that during these duels it is not uncommon for a student to slice off the nose of his adversary, and lay it on the table until the duel is over. After that the surgeon puts it on with mucilage and it never misses a meal, but keeps right on growing.

The wax nose is attractive, but in a warm room it is apt to get excited and wander down into the mustache, or it may stray away under the collar, and when the proprietor goes to wipe this feature he does not wipe anything but space. A gold nose that opens on one side and is engraved, with hunter case and key wind, is attractive, especially on a bright day. The coin-silver nose is very well in its way, but rather commonplace unless designed to match the tea service and the knives and forks. In that case, good taste is repaid by admiration and pleasure on the part of the guest.

The *papier-maché* nose is durable and less liable to become cold and disagreeable. It is also lighter and not liable to season crack.

False noses are made of *papier-maché*, leather, gold, silver and wax. These last are fitted to spectacles or springs, and are difficult to distinguish from a true nose.

Tycho Brahe lost his nose in a duel and wore a golden one, which he attached to his face with cement, which he always carried about.

This was a good scheme, as it found him always prepared for accidents. He could, at any moment, repair to a dressing room, or even slide into an alley where he could avoid the prying gaze of the vulgar world, and glue his nose on. Of course he ran the risk of getting it on crooked and a little out of line with his other features, but this would naturally only attract attention and fix the minds of those with whom he might be called upon to converse. A man with his nose glued on wrong side up, could hold the attention of an audience for hours, when any other man would seem tedious and uninteresting.

SOMETHING TOO MUCH OF THIS.

THE Pawnee Republican, of the 13th, innocently and impertinently, remarks: "Fred Nye, father of Bill Aye, the humorist, is the editor of the Omaha *Republican, vice*Datus Brooks, gone to Europe." — *Omaha Herald.*

Will the press of the country please provide us with a few more parents? Old Jim Nye and several other valuable fathers of ours having already clomb the golden elevator, we now feel like a comparative orphan. The time was when we could hold a reunion of our parents and have a pretty big time, but it's a mighty lonely thing to stand on the shores of time and see your parents whittled down to three or four young men no bigger than Fred Aye, of the *Republican.*

COLOR BLINDNESS.

T HE *Paper World* says there's no use talking, the newspaper men of the press are to-day becoming more and more "color blind." In other words, they have lost that subtle flavor of description for which the public yearns. They have missed that wonderful spice and aroma of narration which is the life of all newspaper work.

We do not take this to ourself at all, but we desire before we say one word, to make a few remarks. *The Boomerang* has been charged with erring on the other side and coloring things a little too high. Sir Garnet Wolseley, in a private letter to us during the late Egyptian assault and battery, stated that if we erred at all it was on the highly colored side.

There is an excuse for lack of spice and all that sort of thing in the newspaper world. The men who write for our dailies, as a rule, have to write about two miles per day, and they ought not to be kicked if it is not as interesting as "Uncle Tom's Cabin," or "Leaves o' Grass."

We have done some 900 miles of writing ourself during our short, sharp and decisive career, and we know what we are talking about. Those things we wrote at a time when we were spreading our graceful characters over ten acres of paper per day, were not thrilling. They did not catch the public eye, but were just naturally consigned to oblivion's bottomless maw.

Read that last sentence twice; it will do you no harm.

The public, it seems to us, has created a false standard of merit for the newspaper. People take a big daily and pay $10 per year for it because it is the biggest paper in the world, and then don't read a quarter of it. They are doing a smart thing, no doubt, but it is killing the feverish young men with throbbing brains, who are doing the work. Would you consider that a large pair of shoes or a large wife should be sought for just because you can get more material for the same price? Not much, Mary Ann!

Excellence is what we seek, not bulk. Write better things and less of them, and you will do better, and the public will be pleased to see the change.

Should anyone who reads these words be suffering from an insatiable hunger for a paper that aims at elegance of diction, high-toned logic and pink cambric sentiment, at a moderate price, he will do well to call at this office and look over our goods. Samples sent free on application, to any part of the United States or Europe. We refer to Herbert Spencer, the Laramie National Bank, and the postmaster of this city, as to our reputation for truth and veracity.

A LITTLE PREVIOUS.

SPEAKING of elections and returns, brings back to our memory the time when it was pretty close in a certain congressional district in Wisconsin, where W. T. Price is now putting up a job on the Democrats.

In those days returns didn't come in by telegraph, but on horseback and on foot, and it was annoying to wait for figures by which to determine the result. At Hudson the politicians had made a pretty close estimate, but were waiting, one evening after election, at a saloon on Buckeye street, for something definite from Eau Claire county. The session was very dull, and to cheer up the little Spartan hand some one suggested that old Judge Wetherby ought to "set 'em up." Judge Wetherby was a staunch old Democrat and had rigidly treated himself for twenty years, and just as rigidly refused to treat anybody else. The result was that he had secured a vigorous bloom on his own nose, but had never put the glass to his neighbor's lips. He intimated on this occasion, however, that if he could get encouraging news from Eau Claire for the Democrats, he would turn loose. The party waited until midnight, and had just decided to go home, when a travel-worn horseman rode up to the door. He was very reticent, and as he was a stranger, no one seemed to want to open up a conversation with him, till at last Judge Wetherby, who couldn't keep the great question of politics out of his mind, asked him what part of the country he had come from. "Just got in from Eau Claire county," was the reply.

"How did Eau Claire county go?" was the Judge's next question. "O, I don't pay no attention to politics, but they told me it went 453 majority for the Democrats."

Thereupon the judge threw his hat in the air and for the first and last time in his life, treated the entire crowd of Republicans and Democrats alike. It was very late when he went home, also very late when he got down town the next day.

When he did come down he was surprised to find a Republican brass band out, and the news all over the city that the Republican candidate had been elected by several hundred majority. In the afternoon he learned that Hod Taylor, now clergyman to Marseilles, had hired a tramp to ride into the Buckeye saloon the previous evening and report as stated, in order to bring about a good state of feeling on the Judge's part. Judge Wetherby, since that time, is regarded as the most skeptical Democrat in that congressional district, and even if he were to be assured over and over again that his party was victorious, he would still doubt. It is such things as these that go a long way toward encouraging a feeling of distrust between the parties, and causes politicians to be looked upon with great mistrust..

Although Mr. Taylor is now in France attending to the affairs of his government, and trying to become familiar with the French language, he often pauses in his work as the memory of this little incident comes over his mind, and a hot tear falls on the report he is making out to send on to the Secretary of State at Washington. Can it be that his hard heart is at last touched with remorse?

IS DUELING MURDER?

SOMEBODY wants to know whether dueling is murder, and we reply in clarion tones that it depends largely on how fatal it is. Dueling with monogram note paper, at a distance of 1,200 yards, is not murder.

HEAP GONE.

ANOTHER land-mark of Laramie has gone. Another wreck has been strewn upon the sands of time. Another gay bark has gone to pieces upon the cruel rocks, and above the broken spars and jib-boom, and foretop gallant royal mainbrace, and spanker-boom euchre deck, the cold, damp tide is moaning.

We refer to L. W. Shroeder, who recently left this place incog., also in debt, largely, to various people of this gay and festive metropolis.

Laramie has been the home, at various times, of some of the most classical dead-beats of modern times; but Shroeder was the noblest, the most grand and co-lossal of dead-beats that has ever visited our shores. Born with unusual abilities in this direction, he early learned how to enlarge and improve upon the talents thus bestowed upon him, and here in Laramie, he soon won a place at the front as a man who purchased everything and paid for nothing. He had a way of approaching the grocer and the merchant that was well calculated to deceive, and he did, in several instances, make representations, which we now learn, were false.

He was, by profession, a carpenter and joiner, having learned the art while cutting cordwood on the Missouri bottoms, near Omaha, for the Collins Brothers. Here he rapidly won his way to the front rank, by erecting some of the most commanding architectural ruins of which modern wood assassination can boast. He would take a hatchet and a buck-saw and carve out his fortune anywhere in the world, and it wouldn't cost him a cent. He filled this whole trans-Missouri country with his fame, and his promissory notes, and then skinned out and left us here to mourn.

Good-bye, Shroeder. Wherever you go, we will remember you and hope that you may succeed in piling up a monument of indebtedness as you did here. You were industrious and untiring in your efforts to become a great financial wreck, and success has crowned your efforts. We will not grudge you the glory that coagulates about your massive brow.

THE EDITORIAL LAMP.

THERE is something unique about an editor's lamp that, enables most any-one to select it from a large number of other lamps. It is *sui generis* and extremely original. The large metropolitan papers use gas in the editorial rooms, and make up for the loss of the kerosene lamp by furnishing their offices with some other article of furniture that is equally attractive.

The Boomerang lamp, especially during the election, has had its intensity wonderfully softened and toned down through various causes. You can take most any other lamp and trim the wick so that it will burn squarely and not smoke; but the editorial lamp is peculiar in this respect. The wick gets so it will burn straight when you find that it does not burn the oil. Then you get it filled and put in a new wick. Experimenting with this you get your fingers perfumed with coal oil, and spill some in your lap. Then you turn it up so you can see, and as you get a flow of thought you look up to find that you have smutted up your chimney, and you murmur something that you are glad no one is near to hear. When our life-record is made up and handed down to posterity, if a generous people will kindly over-look the remarks we have made over our lamp, and also the little extemporaneous statements made at picnics, we will do as much for the public and make this thing as near even as possible.

DIFFICULT TO IDENTIFY.

A DEAD fisherman was taken to the San Francisco morgue the other day, with nothing by which to identify him but his fish fine. There may be features of difference between fish lines, but as a rule there is a long, tame sweep of monotony about them which confuses the authorities in tracing a man's antecedents.

THE MAROON SAUSAGE.

THE maroon sausage will be in favor this winter, as was the case last season in our best circles. It will be caught up at the end and tied in a plain knot with strings of the same.

TESTIMONIALS OF REGARD.

FRIDAY was a large day in the office of this paper. A delegation, consisting of Ed. Walsh and J. J. Clarke, train dispatchers of this division of the Union Pacific road, waited on the editor hereof with two tokens of their esteem. One, consisting of a bird that had been taxidermed at Wyoming station by the agent, Mr. Gulliher, the great corn-canner of the west, aided by another man who has, up to this date, evaded the authorities. As soon as he is captured, his name will be given to the public. The bird is mainly constructed on the duck plan, with web feet and spike tail. The material gave out, however, and the artist was obliged to complete the bird by putting an eagle's head on him. This gives the winged king of birds a low, squatty and plebian cast of countenance, and bothers the naturalist in determining its class and in diagnosing the case. With the piercing, keen eye of the eagle, and the huge Roman nose peculiar to that bird, coupled with the pose of the duck, we have a magnificent combination in the way of an ornithological specimen. Science would be tickled to death to wrestle with this feathered anomaly.

The eagle looks as though he would like to soar first-rate if it were not for circumstances over which he has no control, while the other portions of his person would suggest that he would be glad to paddle around an hour or two in the yielding-mud. We have placed this singular circumstance where he can look down upon us in a reproachful way, while we write abstruse articles upon the contiguity of the hence.

The same committee also presented a bottle of what purported to be ginger ale. It was wrapped up in a newspaper, and the cork was held in place by a piece of copper wire. As we do not drink anything whatever now, we presented it to the composing room, and told the boys to sail in and have a grand debauch.

Generosity is always rewarded, sooner or later. The office boy took it into the composing room and partially opened it. Then it opened itself, with a loud report that shook the dome of *The Boomerang* office, and pied a long article on yellow fever in Texas. Almost immediately after it opened itself, it escaped into space. At least it filled the space box of one of the cases full.

There was only about a spoonful left in the bottle, and no one felt as though he wanted to rob the rest, so it stands there yet. If Mr. Gulliher could put up his goods in such shape as to avoid this high degree of effervescence, he would succeed; but in canning corn and bottling beer, he has so far put too much vigor into the goods, and when you open them, they escape almost immediately.

While we are grateful for the kind and thoughtful spirit shown, we regret that we were unable to test the merits of the beverage without collecting it from the sky, where it now is.

It looks to us as though some day Mr. Gulliher, while engaged in canning and bottling some of his gaseous goods, would be lifted over into the middle of the holidays, and we warn him against being too reckless, or he will certainly meander through the atmosphere sometime, and the place that knew him once will know him no more forever.

About two o'clock the following special was received:

[Special to the Boomerang.]
"[D. H. acct. charity.]
"Wyoming, October 27.

"Dear Bill Nye:

"We made the run from Laramie to Wyoming in one hour. Gulliher says, do not open that bottle; it might go off. He sent you the wrong bottle by mistake. It is a preparation for annihilating tramps, and produces instant dissolution. We, after careful inquiry and rigid investigation, find that the bird is filled with dynamite, nitroglycerine, etc.—in fact is an 'infernal machine,' and is set to go off at 3:30 this P.M."

THE CHINESE COMPOSITOR.

THE Chinese compositor cannot sit at his case as our printers do, but must walk from one case to another constantly, as the characters needed cover such a large number, that they cannot be put into anything like the space used in the English newspaper office. In setting up an ordinary piece of manuscript, the Chinese printer will waltz up and down the room for a few moments, and then go down stairs for a line of lower case. Then he takes the elevator and goes up into the third story after some caps, and then goes out into the woodshed for a handful of astonishers.

The successful Chinese compositor doesn't need to be so very intelligent, but he must be a good pedestrian. He may work and walk around over the building all day to set up a stick full, and then half the people in this county couldn't read it, after all.

"Clarke, Potter and Walsh."

SNOWED UNDER.

W E have met the enemy, and we are his'n.

We have made our remarks, and we are now ready to listen to the gentleman from New York. We could have dug out, perhaps, and explained about New York, but when almost every state in the Union rose up and made certain statements yesterday, we found that the job of explaining this matter thoroughly, would be wearisome and require a great deal of time.

We do not blame the Democracy for this. We are a little surprised, however, and grieved. It will interfere with our wardrobe this winter. With an overcoat on Wyoming, a plug hat on Iowa, a pair of pantaloons on Pennsylvania, and boots on the general result, it looks now as though we would probably go through the winter wrapped in a bed-quilt, and profound meditation.

We intended to publish an extra this morning, but the news was of such a character, that we thought we would get along without it. What was the use of publishing an extra with a Republican majority only in Red Buttes.

The cause of this great Democratic freshet in New York yesterday—but why go into details, we all have an idea why it was so. The number of votes would seem to indicate that there was a tendency toward Democracy throughout the State.

Now, in Pennsylvania, if you will look over the returns carefully—but why should we take up your valuable time offering an explanation of a political matter of the past.

Under the circumstances some would go and yield to the soothing influences of the maddening bowl, but we do not advise that. It would only furnish temporary relief, and the recoil would be unpleasant.

We resume our arduous duties with a feeling of extreme *ennui*, and with that sense of surprise and astonishment that a man does who has had a large brick block fall on him when he was not expecting it. Although we feel a little lonely to-day—having met but a few Republicans on the street, who were obliged to come out and do their marketing—we still hope for the future.

The grand old Republican party—

But that's what we said last week. It sounds hollow now and meaningless, somehow, because our voice is a little hoarse, and we are snowed under so deep that it is difficult for us to enunciate.

Now about those bets. If the parties to whom we owe bets—and we owe most everybody—will just agree to take the stakes, and not go into details; not stop to ask us about the state of our mind, and talk about how it was done, we don't care. We don't wish to have this thing explained at all. We are not of an inquiring turn of mind. Just plain facts are good enough for us, without any harrowing details. In the meantime we are going to work to earn some more money to bet on the next election. Judge Folger, and others, come over and see us when you have time, and we will talk this matter over. Mr. B. Butler, we wish we had your longevity. With a robust constitution, we find that most any man can wear out cruel fate and get there at last. We do not feel so angry as we do grieved and surprised. We are pained to see the American people thus betray our confidence, and throw a large wardrobe into the hands of the relentless foe.

ROUGH ON OSCAR.

SOMEBODY shook a log-cabin bed-quilt at Oscar Wilde, when he was in this country, and it knocked him so crazy for two days, that a man had to lead him around town by a bed-cord to prevent him from butting his head against a lump of oat-meal mush, and scattering his brains all over the Union.

THE POSTAL CARD.

No one denies that the postal card is a great thing, and yet it makes most people mad to get one This is because we naturally feel sensitive about having our correspondence open to the eye of the postmaster and postal clerk. Yet they do not read them. Postal employés hate a postal card as cordially as anyone else. If they were banished and had nothing to read but a package of postal cards, or a foreign book of statistics, they would read the statistics. This wild hunger for postal cards on the part of postmasters is all a myth. When the writer don't care who sees his message, that knocks the curiosity out of those who handle those messages. A man who would read a postal card without being compelled to by some stringent statute, must be a little deranged. When you receive one, you say, "Here's a message of so little importance that the writer didn't care who saw it. I don't care much for it, myself." Then you look it over and lay it away and forget it. Do you think that the postmaster is going to wear out his young life in devouring literature that the sendee don't feel proud of when he receives it? Hay, nay.

During our official experience we have been placed where we could have read postal cards time and again, and no one but the All-seeing Eye would have detected it; but we have controlled ourself and closed our eyes to the written message, refusing to take advantage of the confidence reposed in us by our government, and those who thus trusted us with their secrets. All over our great land every moment of the day or night these little cards are being silently scattered, breathing loving words inscribed with a hard lead pencil, and shedding information upon sundered hearts, and they are as safe as though they had never been breathed.

They are safer, in most instances, because they cannot be read by anybody in the whole world.

That is why it irritates us to have some one open up a conversation by saying, "You remember what that fellow wrote me from Cheyenne on that postal card of the 25th, and how he rounded me up for not sending him those goods?" Now we can't keep all those things in our head. It requires too much of a strain to do it on the salary we receive. A man with a very large salary and a tenacious memory might keep run of the postal correspondence in a small office, but we cannot do it. We are not accustomed to it, and it rattles and excites us.

A CARD.

I HAVE just received a letter from my friend, Bill Nye, of The Laramie City Boomerang, wherein he informs me that he is engaged to the beautiful and accomplished Lydia E. Pinkham, of "Vegetable Compounds" fame, and that the wedding will take place on next Christmas. To be sure, I am expected at the wedding, and I'll be on hand, if I can secure a clean shirt by that time, and the roads ain't too bad. But I'm somewhat at a loss what to get as a suitable present, as Bill informs me in a postscript to his letter, that gifts of bibles, albums, nickel-plated pickle dishes, chromos with frames, and the like, will not be in order, as it is utterly impossible to pawn articles of this kind in Laramie City. — *The Bohemian.*

We are sorry that the above letter, which we dashed off in a careless moment, has been placed before the public, as later developments have entirely changed the aspect of the matter; the engagement between ourself and Lydia having been rudely broken by the young lady herself. She has returned the solitaire filled ring, and henceforth we can be nothing more to each other than friends. The promise which bade fair to yield so much joy in the future has been ruthlessly yanked asunder, and two young hearts must bleed through the coming years. Far be it from us to say aught that would reflect upon the record of Miss Pinkham.

It would only imperil her chances in the future, and deny her the sweet satisfaction of gathering in another guileless sucker like us. The truth, however, cannot be evaded, that Lydia is no longer young. She is now in the sere and yellow leaf. The gurgle of girlhood, and the romping careless grace of her childhood, are matters of ancient history alone.

We might go on and tell how one thing brought on another, till the quarrel occurred, and hot words and an assault and battery led to this estrangement, but we will not do it. It would be wrong for a great, strong man to take advantage of his strength and the public press, to speak disparagingly of a young thing like Lyd. No matter how unreasonably she may have treated us, we are dumb and silent on this point. Journalists who have been invited, and have purchased costly wedding presents, may ship the presents *by* express, prepaid, and we will accept them, and struggle along with our first great heart trouble, while Lydia goes on in her mad career.

WHY WE ARE NOT GAY.

IT was the policy of this paper, from its inception, whatever that is, to frown upon and discourage fraud wherever the latter has shown its hideous front. In doing so, we have simply done our duty, and our reward has been great, partially in the shape of money, and partially in the shape of conscious rectitude and new subscribers.

We shall continue this course until we are able to take a trip to Europe, or until some large man comes into the office with a masked battery and blows us out through the window into the mellow haze of an eternal summer time.

We have been waiting until the present time for about 100,000 shade trees in this town to grow, and as they seem to be a little reluctant about doing so, and the season being now far advanced, we feel safe in saying that they are dead. They were purchased a year ago of a nursery that purported to be O. K., and up to that time no one had ever breathed a word against it. Now, however, unless those trees are replaced, we shall be compelled to publish the name of that nursery in large, glaring type, to the world. The trees looked a little under the weather when they arrived, but we thought we could bring them out by nursing them. They stood up in the spring breeze like a seed wart, however, and refused to leave. They are still obstinate. The agent concluded to leave, but the trees did not. We feel hurt about it, because people come here from a distance and laugh at our hoe-handle forest. They speak jeeringly of our wilderness of deceased elms, and sneer at our defunct magnolias. We hate to cast a reflection on the house, but we also dislike to be played for Chinamen when we are no such thing.

We prefer to sit in the shade of the luxuriant telegraph pole, and stroll at set of sun amid the umbrageous shadows of the barbed wire fence, through which the sunlight glints and glitters to and fro.

Nothing saddens us like death in any form, and 100,000 dead trees scattered through the city, sticking their limbs up into the atmosphere like a variety actress, bears down upon us with the leaden weight of an ever-present gloom.

SCIENTIFIC.

THE Boomerang reporter, sent ont to find the North Pole, eighteen months ago, has just been heard from. An exploring party recently found portions of his remains in latitude 4-11-44, longitude sou'est by sou' from the pole, and near the remains the following fragment of a diary:

July 1,1881.—Have just been out searching for a sunstroke and signs of a thaw. Saw nothing but ice floe and snow as far as the eye could reach. Think we will have snow this evening unless the wind changes.

July 2.—Spent the forenoon exploring to the northwest for right of way for a new equatorial and North Pole railroad that I think would be of immense value to commerce. The grade is easy, and the expense would be slight. Ate my last dog to-day. Had intended him for the 4th, but got too hungry, and ate him raw with vinegar; I wish I was at home eating Boomerang paste.

July 3.—We had quite a frost last night, and it looks this morning as though the corn and small fruits must have suffered. It is now two weeks since the last of the crew died and left me alone. Ate the leather ends of my suspenders to-day for dinner. I did not need the suspenders, anyway, for by tightening up my pants I find they will stay on all right, and I don't look for any ladies to call, so that even if my pants came off by some oversight or other, nobody would be shocked.

July 4.—Saved up some tar roofing and a bottle of mucilage for my Fourth of July dinner, and gorged myself to-day. The exercises were very poorly attended and the celebration rather a failure. It is clouding up in the west, and I'm afraid we're going to have snow. Seems to me we're having an all-fired late spring here this year.

July 5.—Didn't drink a drop yesterday. It was the quietest Fourth I ever put in. I never felt so little remorse over the way I celebrated as I do to-day. I didn't do a thing yesterday that I was ashamed of except to eat the remainder of a box of shoe blacking for supper. To-day I ate my last boot-heel, stewed. Looks as though we might have a hard winter.

July 6.—Feel a little apprehension about something to eat. My credit is all right here, but there is no competition, and prices are therefore very high. Ice, however, is still firm. This would be a good ice-cream country if there were any demand, but the country is so sparsely settled that a man feels as lonesome here as a green-backer at a presidential election. Ate a pound of cotton waste soaked in machine oil, to-day. There is nothing left for to-morrow but ice-water and an old pocket-book for dinner. Looks as though we might have snow.

July 7.—This is a good, cool place to spend the summer if provisions were more plenty. I am wearing a seal-skin undershirt with three woolen overshirts and two bear-skin vests, to-day, and when the dew begins to fall, I have to put on my buffalo ulster to keep off the night air. I wish I was home. It seems pretty lonesome here since the other boys died. I do not know what I will get for dinner to-morrow, unless the neighbors bring in something. A big bear is coming down the hatchway, as I write. I wish I could eat him. It would be the first square meal for two months. It is, however, a little mixed whether I will eat him or he eat me. It will be a cold day for me if he— — — — —"

* * * * *

Here the diary breaks off abruptly, and from the chewed up appearance of the book, we are led to entertain a horrible fear as to his safety.

SCIENTIFIC.

Fourth of July at the North Pole.

THE REVELATION RACKET IN UTAH.

OUR esteemed and extremely connubial contemporary, the *Deseret News*, says in a recent editorial:

"The Latter day Saints will rejoice to learn that the' vacancies which have existed in the quorums of the twelve apostles and the first seven presidents of seventies are now filled. During the conference recently held, Elder Abram H. Cannon was unanimously chosen to be one of the first seven presidents of seventies, and he was ordained to that office on Monday, October 9th. Subsequently, the Lord, by revelation through His servant, Prest. John Taylor, designated by name, Brothers George Teasdale and Heber J. Grant, to be ordained to the apostleship, and Brother Seymour B. Young to fill the remaining vacancy in the presidency of the seventies. These brethren were ordained on Monday, October 16th, the two apostles, under the hands of the first presidency and twelve, and the other under the hands of the twelve and the presidency of the seventies."

Now, that's a convenient system of politics and civil service. When there is a vacancy, the president, John Taylor, goes into his closet and has a revelation which settles it all right. If the man appointed vicariously by the Lord is not in every way satisfactory, he may be discharged by the same process. Instead, therefore, of being required to rally a large force of his friends to aid him in getting an appointment, the aspirant arranges solely with the party who runs the revelation business. It will be seen at a glance, therefore, that the man who can get the job of revelating in Zion, has it pretty much his own way. We would not care who made the laws of Utah if we could do its revelating at so much per revelate.

Think of the power it gives a man in a community of blind believers. Imagine, if you please, the glorious possibilities in store for the man who can successfully reveal the word of the Lord in an easy, extemporaneous manner on five minutes notice.

This prerogative does not confine itself to politics alone. The impromptu revelator of the Jordan has revelations when he wants to evade the payment of a bill. He gets a divine order also if he desires to marry a beautiful maid or seal the new school ma'am to himself. He has a leverage which he can bring to bear upon the people of his diocese at all times, even more potent than the press, and it does not possess the drawbacks that a newspaper does. You can run an aggressive paper if you want to in this country, and up to the time of the funeral you have a pretty active and enjoyable time, but after the grave has been filled up with the clods of the valley and your widow has drawn her insurance, you naturally ask, "What is the advantage to be gained by this fearless style of journalism?"

Still, even the inspired racket has its drawbacks. Last year, a little incident occurred in a Mormon family down in southern Utah, which weighed about nine pounds, and when the *ex officio* husband, who had been absent two years, returned, he acted kind of wild and surprised, somehow, and as he went through the daily round of his work he could be seen counting his fingers back and forth and looking at the almanac, and adding up little amounts on the side of the barn with a piece of red chalk.

Finally, one of the inspired mob of that part of the vineyard thought it was about time to get a revelation and go down there, so he did so. He sailed up to the *de facto* husband and *quasi* parent and solemnly straightened up some little irregularities as to dates, but the revelation was received with disdain, and the revelator was sent home in an old ore sack and buried in a peach basket.

Sometimes there is, even in Utah, a manifestation of such irreverence and open hostility to the church that it makes us shudder.

SAGE BRUSH TONIC.

W E have a scheme on hand which we believe will be even more remuner-ative than the newspaper business, if successfully carried out. It is to construct a national remedy and joy-to-the-world tonic, composed of the carefully expressed juice of our Rocky mountain tropical herb, known as the sage brush. Sage brush is known to possess wonderful medicinal properties. It is bitter enough to act as a tonic and to convey the idea of great strength. Our idea would be to have our portrait on each bottle, to attract attention and aid in effecting a cure. We have noticed that the homeliest men succeed best as patent medicine inventors, and this would be right in our hand.

The tonic could be erected at a cost of three cents per bottle, delivered on the cars here, and after we got fairly to going we might probably reduce even that price. At one dollar per bottle, we could realize a living profit, and still do mankind a favor and turn loose a boon to suffering humanity. It will make the hair grow, as everyone knows, and it will stir up a torpid liver equally well. It just loves to get after anything that is dormant. It might even help the Democratic party, if it had a chance.

Our plan would be to advertise liberally, for we know the advantages of judicious advertising. Only last week a man on South C street had three cows to sell, which fact he set forth in this paper at the usual rates. Before he went to bed that evening the cows were sold and people were filing in the front gate like a row of men at the general delivery of the postoffice. The next morning a large mob of people was found camped out in front of the house, and the railroad was giving excursion rates to those who wanted to come in from the country to buy these cows that had been sold the day before.

We just quote this to show how advertising stirs the mighty deep and wakes people up. We would make propositions to our brethren of the press by which they could make some money out of the ad, too, instead of telling them to put it in the middle of the telegraph page, surrounded by pure reading matter, daily and weekly till forbid and pay when we get ready.

Publishers will find that we are not that kind of people. We shall aim to do the square thing, and will throw in an electrotype, showing us just discovering the sage brush, and exclaiming "Eureka," while we prance around like a Zulu on the war path. Underneath this we will write, "Yours for Health," or words to that effect, and everything will be pleasant and nice.

The Sage Brush Tonic will be made of two grades, one will be for prohibition states and the other for states where prohibition is not in general use. The prohibition tonic will contain, in addition to the sage brush, a small amount of tansy and Jamaica ginger, to give it a bead and prevent it from fermenting. A trial bottle will be sent to subscribers of this paper, also a fitting little poem to be read at the funeral. We will also publish death notice of those using the tonic, at one-half rates.

LAME FROM HIS BERTH.

A SAD-EYED man, the other night, fell out of his bed into the aisle of a Pullman car and skinned his knee. He now claims that he was lame from his berth. When he passes Carbon he will be hung by request.

THE PUBLIC PRINTER.

VERY few of the great mass of humanity know who makes the beautiful public document, with its plain, black binding and wealth of statistics. Few stop to think that hidden away from the great work-a-day world, with eyelids heavy and red, and with finger-nails black with antimony, toiling on at his case hour after hour, the public printer, during the sessions of Congress, is setting up the thrilling chapters of the Congressional Record, and between times yanking the Washington press backward and forward, with his suspenders hanging down, as he prints this beautiful sea-side library of song.

We are too prone to read that which gives us pleasure without thought of the labor necessary to its creation. We glide gaily through the Congressional Record, pleased with its more attractive features, viz: its ayes and noes—little recking that Sterling P. Rounds, the public printer, stands in the subdued gaslight with his stick half full, trying to decipher the manuscript of some reticent representative, whose speech was yesterday delivered to the janitor as he polished the porcelain cuspidor of Congress.

This is a day and age of the world when men take that which comes to them, and do not stop to investigate the pain and toil it costs. They never inquire into the mystery of manufacture, or try to learn the details of its construction. Most of our libraries are replete with books which we have received at the hands of a generous government, and yet we treat those volumes with scorn and contumely. We jeer at the footsore bugologist who has chased the large, green worm from tree to tree, in order that we may be wise. We speak sneeringly of the man who stuffs the woodtick, and paints the gaudy wings of the squash-bug that we may know how often she orates.

Year after year the entomologist treads the same weary road with his bait-box tied to his waist, wooing to his laboratory the army-worm and the sheep-scab larvæ in order that we, poor particles on the surface of the great earth, may know how these minute creatures rise, flourish and decay.

Then the public printer throws in his case, rubs his finger and thumb over a lump of alum, takes a chew of tobacco, and puts in type these words of wisdom from the lips of gray-bearded savants, that knowledge may be scattered over the broad republic. Patiently he goes on with the click of type, anon in an absorbed way, while we, gay, thoughtless mortals, wear out the long summer day at a basket picnic, with deft fingers selecting the large red ant from our cold ham.

Thus these books are made which come to us wrapped in manilla and frank-ed by the man we voted for last fall. Beautiful lithographs, illustrating the differ-ent stages of hog cholera, deck their pages. Rich oil paintings of gaudy tobacco worms chase each other from preface to errata. Magnificent chromos of the foot and mouth disease appeal to us from page after page, and statistics boil out be-tween them, showing what per cent of invalid or convalescent animals was sent abroad, and what per cent was worked into oleomargarine and pressed corn beef.

And what becomes of all this wealth of information—this mammoth aggrega-tion of costly knowledge?

Cast ruthlessly away by a trifling, shallow, frivolous and freckle-minded race!

It is no more than right that Sterling P. Rounds should know this. How it will gall his proud heart to know how his beautiful books, and his chatty and spicy Congressional Record are treated by a jeering, heartless throng! Do you sup-pose that I would perspire over doubtful copy night after night, and then tread a job printing press all the next day printing books at which the bloodless, soulless public sneered, and the broad-browed talent of a cruel generation spit upon? Not exactly.

I have a moderate amount of patience and self-control, but I am free to say right here before the world, that if I had been in Mr. Rounds' place, and had at great cost erected a scientific work upon "The Rise and Fall of Botts in America," and a flippant nation of scoffers had utilized that volume to press autumn leaves and scraggly ferns in, I would rise in my proud might and mash the forms with a mallet, I would jerk the lever of the Washington press into the middle of the efful-gent hence. I would kick over my case, wipe the roller on the frescoed walls, and feed my statistics, to the hungry flames.

No publisher has ever been treated more shabbily; no compositor has, in the history of literature, been more rudely disregarded and derided.

Think of this, dear reader, when you look carelessly over the brief but wonder-ful career of the hop-louse, or with apparent *ennui* dawdle through the treatise on colic among silk-worms, and facial neuralgia among fowls.

This will not only please Mr. Rounds, the young and struggling compositor, but it will gratify and encourage all the friends of American progress and the lov-ers of learning throughout our whole land.

A REPRODUCTIVE COMET.

AN exchange remarks: "The present comet in the eastern sky, which can be distinctly seen by everyone at early morning, is certainly the most remarkable one of the modern comets. Professor Lewis Swift, director of the Warner observatory, Rochester, New York, states that the comet grazed the sun so closely as to cause great disturbance, so much so, that it has divided into no less than eight separate parts, all of which can be distinctly seen by a good telescope. There is only one other instance on record, where a comet has divided, that one being Biella's comet of 1846, which separated into two parts. Applications have been made to Mr. H. H. Warner, by parties who have noticed these cometary offshoots, claiming the $200 prize for each one of them. Whether the great comet will continue to produce a brood of smaller comets remains to be seen."

It is certainly to be hoped that it will not. If the comet is going to multiply and replenish the earth, the average inhabitant had better proceed in the direction of the tall timber.

It excites and rattles us a good deal now to look out for what comets we have on hand; but that is mild, compared with what we will experience if the heavens are to be filled every spring with new laid comets, and comets that haven't got their eyes open yet. Our astronomers are able to figure on the old parent comets, and they know when to look for them, too; but if twins are to burst upon our vision occasionally, and little bob-tail orphan comets are to float around through space, we will have to kind of get up and seek out another solar system, where we will be safe from this comet foundling asylum.

Instead of the calm sky of night, flooded with the glorious effulgence of the silvery moon, surrounded by the twinkling stars, the coming sky will be one grand Fourth of July exhibit of fireworks, with a thousand little disobedient comets coming from the four corners of heaven in search of the milky way.

Possibly science may be wrong. We have known science to make bad little breaks of that kind, and when it advertised a particular show to come off, it was delayed by a wreck on the main track, or something of that kind, so that people were disappointed. Let us hope that this is the case now, and that the comets now loafing around through space with their coat tails on fire will not become parents. It would be scandalous.

A LITTLE VAGUE.

A TALL, pleasant-looking gentleman, with quick, restless eyes, and the air of a man who had been in a newspaper office before, dropped into The Boomerang science department yesterday, and asked the pale, scholarly blossom, who sat writing an epic on the alarming prevalence of pip and its future as a national evil, if he could be permitted to read the *Deseret News*.

The scientist said certainly, and after a long and weary tussle got the Mormon placque out of the ruins.

"I used to be foreman on the *Deseret News*," said the gentleman with the penetrating eye; "I worked on the News two years, and had a case on the *Tribune*. I've been foreman of thirty-seven papers during my life, but my most unfortunate experience was on the *Deseret News*. I wanted the paper just now to see if they were still running an ad. that I had some trouble with when I was there.

"It was a contract we had with Dr. Balshazzer to advertise his Blue Eyed Forget-me Not Perfume, Dr. Balshazzer's Red Tar Worm Buster, and Dr. Balshazzer's Baled Brain Food and Tolurockandryeandcodliveroil. The Blue Eyed Forget-me Not Perfume was to go solid in long primer, following pure reading matter eod in daily and eowtf weekly. The Red Tar Worm Buster was to go in nonpareil leaded, 192I.T.thFth98weow3mo, and repeat; and the Baled Brain Food and Tolurock-andryecodliveroil was a six-inch electrotype to go in on third page, following pure original humorous matter, with six full head lines d&weod oct9tf, set in reading type similar to copy; these to be inserted between pure religious news, with no other advertising within four miles of the electro, or the reading notices.

"At the same time we were running old Monkeywrench's Kidney Scraper on the same kind of a contract. The business manager did not remember this when we took the contract, so that as soon as we began to run the two there was a collision between the Tolurockandryeandcodliver-oil and the Kidney Scraper right off. I spoke to the business manager about it, and he was puzzled. He didn't exactly know what it was best to do under the circumstances, and he hated to lose old Balshazzer's whole trade, for he wouldn't run any of his ads unless he would take them all according to his contract.

"We tried to get him to let us run the BlueEyed Forget-me Not Perfume, lapr9d&wly deod&wly 10:2t-eowtf; the Bed Tar Worm Buster, dol3 4t da22tf apr-lo-ly dol3tf, and the Brain Food and Tolurockandryecodliveroil mchl8*ly jun4dt-f&dangl8@gft>*&Sylds30tf&rsvpeod$, but he wouldn't do it.

"I displayed his ad. top of column adjoining humorous column with three line readers and astonishers without advertising marks or signs according to copy and instructions to foreman, all omissions or errors to be subject to fine and imprisonment. They were to go pdq $eoy*Octp&s* and they were to be double leaded and headed with italic caps. Still I said it had been some time since I saw the contract and I had been suffering with brain fever six months in jail and possibly my memory might be defective. I would go over it again and see if I was right.

"The electrophones were to be blown in the bottle and the readers were to be set in lower case slugs with guarantee of good faith and Rough on Rats would not die in the house. Use Pinkham's Sozodont for itching, freckles, bunions and croup. It saved my life. My good woman, why are you bilious with em quads in solid minion. Eureka Jumbo Baking Powder will not crack or fade in any climate sent on three months trial in leaded brevier quoins and all wool column rules warranted to cure rheumatism and army worms or money refunded. To be adjoining selected miscellany or fancy brass dashes marked eodsyld&w*!*?—" At this moment a dark browed man came in and told us that the young man was his charge and on his way to Mount Pleasant asylum for the insane and that we would have to excuse the intrusion. After subscribing for the paper and asking us if we had heard from Ohio, he went.

The scientist said afterward that he found it difficult to follow the young man in some of his statements and that he was just going to ask him to go over that again and say it slower, when the Mount Pleasant man came in and interrupted the flow of conversation.

SAD DESTRUCTION.

THERE came very near being a holocaust in this office on Monday. An absent-minded candidate for the legislature lit his cigar and gently threw the match in the waste basket. Shortly after that we felt a grateful warmth stealing up our back and melting the rubber in our suspenders. The fire was promptly put under control by our editorial fire department, but the basket is no longer fit to hold a large word.

THE IMMEDIATE REVOLTER.

WYOMING has recently been a great sufferer, mainly through the carrying of revolvers in the caboose of the overalls. There is no more need of carrying a revolver in Wyoming than there is of carrying an upright piano in the coat tail pocket. Those who carry revolvers generally die by the revolver, and he who agitates the six-shooter, by the six-shooter shall his blood be shed. When a man carries a gun he does so because he has said or done something for which he expects to be attacked, so it is safe to say that when a man goes about our peaceful streets, loaded, he has been doing some, little trick or other, and has in advance prepared himself for a Smith-&-Wesson matinee. The other class of men who suffer from the revolver comprises the white-livered and effeminate parties who ought to be arrested for wearing men's clothes, and who never shoot anybody except by accident. Fortunately they sometimes shoot themselves, and then the fool-killer puts his coat on and rests half an hour. We have been writing these things and obituaries alternately for several years, and yet there is no falling off in the mortality. For every man who is righteously slain, there are about a million law-abiding men, women and children murdered. Eternity's parquette is filled with people who got there by the self-cocking revolver route.

A man works twenty years to become known as a scholar, a newspaper man and a gentleman, while the illiterate murderer springs into immediate notoriety in a day, and the widow of his victim cannot even get her life insurance. These things are what make people misanthropic and tenacious of their belief in a hell.

If revolvers could not be sold for less than $500 a piece, with a guarantee on the part of the vendee, signed by good sureties, that he would support the widows and orphans, you would see more longevity lying around loose, and western cemeteries would cease to roll up such mighty majorities.

THE SECRET OF HEALTH.

HEALTH journals are now asserting, that to maintain a sound constitution you should lie only on the right side. The health journals may mean well enough; but what are you going to do if you are editing a Democratic paper?

HOUSEHOLD RECIPES.

TO remove oils, varnishes, resins, tar, oyster soup, currant jelly, and other selections from the bill of fare, use benzine, soap and chloroform cautiously with whitewash brush and garden hose. Then hang on wood pile to remove the pungent effluvia of the benzine.

To clean ceilings that have been smoked by kerosene lamps, or the fragrance from fried salt pork, remove the ceiling, wash thoroughly with borax, turpentine and rain water, then hang on the clothes line to dry. Afterward pulverize and spread over the pie plant bed for spring wear.

To remove starch and roughness from flatirons, hold the iron on a large grindstone for twenty minutes or so, then wipe off carefully with a rag. To make this effective, the grindstone should be in motion while the iron is applied. Should the iron still stick to the goods when in use, spit on it.

To soften water for household purposes, put in an ounce of quicklime in a certain quantity of water. If it is not sufficient, use less water or more quicklime. Should the immediate lime continue to remain deliberate, lay the water down on a stone and pound it with a base ball club.

To give relief to a burn, apply the white of an egg. The yolk of the egg may be eaten or placed on the shirt bosom, according to the taste of the person. If the burn should occur on a lady, she may omit the last instruction.

To wash black silk stockings, prepare a tub of lather, composed of tepid rain water and white soap, with a little ammonia. Then stand in the tub till dinner is ready. Roll in a cloth to dry. Do not wring, but press the water out. This will necessitate the removal of the stockings.

If your hands are badly chapped, wet them in warm water, rub them all over with Indian meal, then put on a coat of glycerine and keep them in your pockets for ten days. If you have no pockets convenient, insert them in the pocket of a friend.

An excellent liniment for toothache or neuralgia, is made of sassafras, oil of organum and a half ounce of tincture of capsicum, with half a pint of alcohol. Soak nine yards of red flannel in this mixture, wrap it around the head and then insert the head in a haystack till death comes to your relief.

To remove scars or scratches from the limbs of a piano, bathe the limb in a solution of tepid water and tincture of sweet oil. Then apply a strip of court plaster, and put the piano out on the lawn for the children to play horse with.

Woolen goods may be nicely washed if you put half an ox gall into two gallons of tepid water. It might be well to put the goods in the water also. If the mixture is not strong enough, put in another ox gall. Should this fail to do the work, put in the entire ox, reserving the tail for soup. The ox gall is comparatively useless for soup, and should not be preserved as an article of diet.

WHAT IS LITERATURE?

A SQUASH-NOSED scientist from away up the creek, asks, "What is literature!" Cast your eye over these logic-imbued columns, you sun-dried savant from the remote precincts. Drink at the never-failing Boomerang springs of forgotten lore, you dropsical wart of a false and erroneous civilization. Read our "Address to the Duke of Stinking Water," or the "Ode to the Busted Snoot of a Shattered Venus DeMilo," if you want to fill up your thirsty soul with high-priced literature. Don't go around hungering for literary pie while your eyes are closed and your capacious ears are filled with bales of hay.

THE PREVIOUS HOTEL.

DOWN at Nathrop, Colorado, there is a large, new, and fine hotel, where no guest ever ate or slept. It stands there near the South Park track like the ghost of some nice, clean country inn. The reader will naturally ask if the house is haunted, that no one stops at the very attractive hotel in a country where good hotels are rare. No, it is not that. It in not haunted so much as it would like to be. Though it is a fine hotel, there is no town nearer it than Buena Vista, and no one is going to do business at Buena Yista and go up to Nathrop on a hand-car for his meals.

It is a case where a smart aleck of a man built a hotel, and asked his fellow citizens to come and form a town around him and make him rich. Mr. Nathrop was rather an impulsive man, and one day he said something that reflected on another impulsive man, and when people came and looked for Nathrop, they found that his body was tangled up in the sage brush, and his soul was marching on.

The hotel was just completed, and the ladders, and the handsome lime barrels, and hods, and old nail kegs, and fragments of laths, and pieces of bricks, and scaffolds, and all those things that go to make life desirable, are still there adorning the hotel and the front yard; but there is no handsome man with a waxed mustache inside at the desk, shaking his head sadly when he is asked for a room, and looking at you with that high-born pity and contempt for your pleading, that the hotel clerk—heir apparent to the universe—always keeps for those who go to him with humility.

There is no Senegambian, with a whisk broom, waiting to brush your clothes off your back, and leave you arrayed in a birth-mark and the earache, at twenty-five cents per brush. There is no young, fair masher, strutting up and down the piazza, trying to look brainy and capable of a thought. It is only a hollow mockery, for the chamber-maid with the large slop-pail does not come at daylight to pound on your door, and try to get in and fix up your room, and wake you up, and frighten you to death with her shocking chaos of wart-environed and freckle-frescoed beauty.

There the new hotel will, no doubt, stand for ages, while a little way off, in his quiet grave, the proprietor, laid to rest in an old linen handkerchief, is sleeping away the years till he shall be awakened by the last grand reveille. There's no use talking, it's tough.

ANECDOTE OF SPOTTED TAIL.

THE popularity of the above-named chieftain dates from a very trifling little incident, as did that of many other men who are now great.

Spotted Tail had never won much distinction up to that time, except as the owner of an appetite, in the presence of which his tribe stood in dumb and terrible awe.

During the early days of what is now the great throbbing and ambitious west, the tribe camped near Fort Sedgwick, and Big Mouth, a chief of some importance, used to go over to the post regularly for the purpose of filling his brindle hide full of "Fort Sedgwick Bloom of Youth."

As a consequence of Big Mouth's fatal yearning for liquid damnation, he generally got impudent, and openly announced on the parade ground that he could lick the entire regular army. This used to offend some of the blood-scarred heroes who had just arrived from West Point, and in the heat of debate they would warm the venerable warrior about two feet below the back of his neck with the fiat of their sabers.

This was a gross insult to Big Mouth, and he went back to the camp, where he found Spotted Tail eating a mule that had died of inflammatory rheumatism. Big Mouth tearfully told the wild epicure of the way he had been treated, and asked for a council of war. Spot picked his teeth with a tent pin, and then told the defeated relic of a mighty race that if he would quit strong drink, he would be subjected to fewer insults.

Big Mouth then got irritated, and told S. Tail that his remarks showed that he was standing, in with the aggressor, and was no friend to his people.

Spotted Tail said that Mr. B. Mouth was a liar, by yon high heaven, and before there was time to think it over, he took a butcher knife, about four feet long, from its scabbard and cut Mr. Big Mouth plumb in two just between the umbilicus and the watch pocket.

As the reader who is familiar with anatomy has already surmised, Big Mouth died from the effects of this wound, and Spotted Tail was at once looked upon as the Moses of his tribe. He readily rose to prominence, and by his strict attention to the duties of his office, made for himself a name as a warrior and a pie biter, at which the world turned pale.

"ANECDOTE OF SPOTTED TAIL."

This should teach us the importance of taking the tide at its flood, which leads on to fortune, and to lay low when there is a hen on, as Benjamin Franklin has so truly said.

THE ZEALOUS VOTER.

SPEAKING of New York politics," said Judge Hildreth, of Cummings, the other day, "they have a cheerful way of doing business in Gotham, and at first it rather surprised me. I went into New York a short time before election, and a Democratic friend told me I had better go and get registered so I could 'wote.' I did so, for I hate to lose the divine right of suffrage, even when I'm a good way from home.

"When election day came around, I went over to the polls in a body, in the afternoon, but they wouldn't let me vote. I told them I was registered all right, and that I had a right and must exercise it the same as any other Democrat in this enlightened land, but they swore at me and entreated me roughly, and told me to go there myself, and that I had already voted once and couldn't do it any more. I had always thought that New York was prone to vigilance and industry in the suffrage business, and early and often was what I supposed was the grand hailing sign. It made me mad, therefore, to have the city get so virtuous all at once that it couldn't even let me vote once.

"I was irritated and extremely ill-natured when I went back to Mr. McGinnis, and told him. of the great trouble I had had with the judges of election, and I denounced New York politics with a great deal of fervor.

"Mr. McGinnis said it was all right.

"'That's aizy enough to me, George. Give me something difficult. Sit down and rist yoursilf. Don't get excited and talk so loud. I know'd yez was out lasht night wid the byes and you didn't feel like gettin' up airly to go to the polls, so I got wan av the byes to go over and wote your name. That's all roight, come here 'nd have someding.'

"I saw at a glance that New York people were attending to these things thoroughly and carefully, and since that when I hear that 'a full vote hasn't been polled in New York city' for some unknown cause, I do not think it is true. I look upon the statement with great reserve, for I believe they vote people there who have been dead for centuries, and people who have not yet arrived in this country, nor even expressed a desire to come over. I am almost positive that they are still voting the bones of old A. T. Stewart up in the doubtful wards, and as soon as Charlie Ross is entitled to vote, he will most assuredly be permitted to represent.

"Why, there's one ward there where they vote the theatre ghosts and the spirit of Hamlet's father hasn't missed an election for a hundred years."

HOW TO PRESERVE TEETH.

I FIND," said an old man to a Boomerang reporter, yesterday, "that there is absolutely no limit to the durability of the teeth, if they are properly taken care of. I never drink hot drinks, always brush my teeth morning and evening, avoid all acids whatever, and although I am 65 years old, my teeth are as good as ever they were."

"And that is all you do to preserve your teeth, is it?"

"Yes, sir; that's all—barring, perhaps, the fact that I put them in a glass of soft water nights."

MR. BEECHER'S BRAIN.

Mr. BEECHER, has raked in $2,000,000 with his brain. A good, tall, bulging brow, and a brain that will give down like that, are rather to be chosen than a blind lead, and an easy running cerebellum, than a stone quarry with a silent but firm skunk in it.

OH, NO!

T HE telephone line between Cheyenne and Laramie City will soon be in operation. It won't work, however. It may be a success for a time, but sooner or later Bill Nye will set his lopsided jaws at work in front of the transmitter, and pour a few quarts of untutored lies into the contribution box, which does service as a part of the telephone machine. Then the wires will be yanked off the poles, a hissing torrent of prevarication will blow the battery jars clean over into Utah, and the listener at the Cheyenne end will be gathered up in a basket. Weeping friends will hold a funeral over a pair of old boots and a fragment of shoulder blade — the remains of the departed Cheyennese. It is a weird and pixycal thing to be a natural born liar, but there are times when a robust lie will successfully defy the unanimous inventive genius of the age." — *Sun*.

Oh, do not say those cruel words, kind friend. Do not throw it up to us that we are weird and pixycal. Oh, believe us, kind sir, we may have done wrong, but we never did that. We know that election is approaching, and all sorts of bygone crookedness is raked up at that time, even when a man is not a candidate for office, but we ask the public to scan our record and see if the charge made by the *Sun* is true. It may be that years ago we escaped justice and fled to the west under an assumed name, but no man ever before charged us with being weird and pixycal. We have been in all kinds of society, perhaps, and mingled with people who were our inferiors, having been pulled by the police once while visiting a Democratic caucus, but that was our misfortune, not our fault. We were not a member of the caucus and were therefore discharged, but even little things like that ought to be forgotten.

As for entering any one's apartments and committing a pixycal crime, we state now without fear of successful contradiction, that it is not so. It is no sign because a man in an unguarded moment entered the Rock Creek eating house and gave way to his emotions, that he is a person to be shunned. It was hunger, and not love for the questionable, that made us go there. It is not because we are by nature weird or pixycal, for we are not. We are not angry over this charge. It just simply hurts and grieves us. It comes too, at a time when we are trying to lead a different life, and while others are trying to lend us every aid and encouragement. We have many friends in Cheyenne who want to see us come up and take higher ground, but how can we do so if the press lends its influence against us. That's just the way we feel about it. If the public prints try to put us down and crush us in this manner, we will probably get desperate and be just as weird and pixycal as we can be.

THE MARCH OF CIVILIZATION.

"SPOKANE IKE," the Indian who killed a doctor last summer for failing to cure his child, has been hanged. This shows the onward march of civilization, and vouchsafes to us the time when a doctor's life will be in less danger than that of his patient.

AN UNCLOUDED WELCOME.

N.P. WILLIS once said: "The sweetest thing in life is the unclouded welcome of a wife." This is true, indeed, but when her welcome is clouded with an atmosphere of angry words and coal scuttles, there is something about it that makes a man want to go out in the woodshed and sleep on the ice-chest.

THE PILLOW-SHAM HOLDER.

SOME enemy to mankind has recently invented an infernal machine known as the pillow-sham holder, which is attached to the head of the bedstead and works with a spiral spring. It is a kind of refined towel-rack on which you hang your pillow-shams at night so they wont get busted by the man of the house. The man of the house generally gets the pillow-shams down under his feet when he undresses and polishes off his cunning little toes on the lace poultice on which his wife prides herself. This pillow-sham holder saves all this. You just yank your pillow-sham off the bed and hang it on this high-toned sham holder, where it rests all night. At least that's the intention. After a little while, however, the spring gets weak, and the holder buckles to, or caves in, or whatever you may call it, at the most unexpected moment. The slightest movement on the part of the occupant of the bed, turns loose the pillow-sham holder, and the slumberer gets it across the bridge of his or her nose, as the case may be. Sometimes the vibration caused by a midnight snore, will unhinge this weapon of the devil, and it will whack the sleeper across the features in a way that scares him almost to death. If you think it is a glad surprise to get a lick across the perceptive faculties in the middle of a sound slumber, when you are dreaming of elysium and high-priced peris and such things as that, just try the death-dealing pillow-sham holder, and then report in writing to the chairman of the executive committee. It is well calculated to fill the soul with horror and amaze. A raven-black Saratoga wave, hanging on the back of a chair, has been known to turn white in a single night as the result of the sudden kerflummix of one of these cheerful articles of furniture.

SOMETHING FRESH.

OUR Saturday dispatches announce that an infernal machine had just been received at the office of Chief Justice Field, and later on, Justice Field, who was in Wyoming Saturday, said to a reporter that the machine was one that was sent to him in 1866, and that last week he sent it down to a gun factory to have the powder taken out, as he wished to stuff it and preserve it among the archives.

With the aid of the telegraph and the facilities of the Associated Press, it does seem as though we were living in an age of almost miraculous possibilities. Here is an instance where an infernal machine is sent to a prominent man, and in less than sixteen years the news is flashed to the four quarters of the globe like lightning. How long will it be before the whole bloody history of the war of the rebellion will be sent to every hamlet in the land? How long before the safe arrival of the ark, and the losses occasioned by the deluge, will be given to us in dollars and cents?

People don't fully realize the advantages we possess in this glorious nine-teenth century. They take all these things as a matter of course, and forget how the palpitating brain palps for them, and how the quivering nerve quivs on and on through the silent night in order that humanity may keep informed in relation to ancient history.

A BAKEFOOTED GODDESS.

THERE'S one little national matter that has been neglected about long enough, it seems to us. If the goddess of liberty is allowed to go barefoot for another century, her delicate toes will spread out over this nation like the shadow of a great woe.

YANKED TO ETERNITY.

ONCE, when a section-crew came down the mountain on the South Park road, from Alpine Tunnel to Buena Vista, a very singular thing occurred, which has never been given to the public. Every one who knows anything at all, knows that riding down that mountain on a push-car, descending at the rate of over 200 feet to the mile, means utter destruction, unless the brake is on. This brake is nothing more nor less then a piece of scantling, which is applied between one of the wheels and the car-bed, in such a way as to produce great friction.

The section-crew referred to, got on at Hancock with their bronzed and glowing hides as full of arsenic and rain-water as they could possibly hold. Being recklessly drunk, they enjoyed the accumulated velocity of the car wonderfully, until the section boss lost the break off the car, and then there was a slight feeling of anxiety. The car at last acquired a velocity like that of a young and frolicsome bob-tailed comet turned loose in space. The boys began to get nervous at last, and asked each other what should be done.

There seemed to be absolutely nothing to do but to shoot onward into the golden presently.

All at once the section boss thought of something. He was drunk, but the deadly peril of the moment suggested an idea. There was a rope on the car which would do to tie to something heavy and cast off for an anchor. The idea was only partially successful, however, for there was nothing to tie to but a spike hammer. This was tried but it wouldn't work. Then it was decided to tie it to some one of the crew and cast him loose in order to save the lives of those who remained. It was a glorious opportunity. It was a heroic thing to do. It was like Arnold Winklered's great sacrifice, by which victory was gained by filling his own system full of lances and making a toothpick holder of himself, in order that his comrades might break through the ranks of their foes.

George O'Malley, the section boss, said that he was willing that Patsy McBride should snatch the laurels from outrageous fortune and bind them on his brow, but Mr. McBride said he didn't care much for the encomiums of the world. He hadn't lost any encomiums, and didn't want to trade his liver for two dollars' worth of damaged laurels.

Everyone declined. All seemed willing to go down into history without any ten-line pay-local, and wanted someone else to get the effulgence. Finally, it was decided that a man by the name of Christian Christianson was the man to tie to.

He had the asthma anyhow, and life wasn't much of an object to him, so they said that, although he declined, he must take the nomination, as he was in the hands of his friends.

So they tied the rope around Christian and cast anchor.

* * * * * *

The car slowed up and at last stopped still. The plan had succeeded. Five happy wives greeted their husbands that night as they returned from the jaws of destruction. Christian Christianson did not return. The days may come and the days may go, but Christian's wife will look up toward the summit' of the snow-crowned mountains in vain.

He will never entirely return. He has done so partially, of course, but there are still missing fragments of him, and it looks as though he must have lost his life.

WHY WE SHED THE SCALDING.

IN justice to ourself we desire to state that the Cheyenne *Sun* has villified us and placed us in a false position before the public. It has stated that while at Rock Creek station, in the early part of the week, we were taken for a peanutter, and otherwise ill-treated at the railroad eating corral and omelette emporium, and that in consequence of such treatment we shed great scalding tears as large as water-melons. This is not true. We did shed the tears as above set forth, but not because of ill-treatment on the part of the eating-house proprietor.

It was the presence of death that broke our heart and opened the fountains of our great deep, so to speak. When we poured the glucose syrup on our pancakes, the stiff and cold remains of a large beetle and two cunning little twin cockroaches fell out into our plate, and lay there hushed in an eternal repose.

Death to us is all powerful. The King of Terrors is to us the mighty sovereign before whom we must all bow, from the mighty emperor down to the meanest slave, from the railroad superintendent, riding in his special car, down to the humblest humorist, all alike must some day curl up and die. This saddens us at all times, but more peculiarly so when Death, with his relentless lawn mower, has gathered in the young and innocent. This was the case where two little twin cockroaches, whose lives had been unspotted, and whose years had been unclouded by wrong and selfishness, were called upon to meet death together. In the stillness of the night, when others slept, these affectionate little twins crept into the glucose syrup and died.

We hope no one will misrepresent this matter. We did weep, and we are not ashamed to own it. We sat there and sobbed until the tablecloth was wet for four feet, and the venerable ham was floating around in tears. It was not for ourself, however, that we wept. No unkindness on the part of an eating-house ever provoked such a tornado of woe. We just weep when we see death and are brought in close contact with it. And we were not the only one that shed tears. Dickinson and Warren wept, strong men as they were. Even the butter wept. Strong as it was it could not control its emotions.

We don't very often answer a newspaper attack, but when we are accused of weeping till people have to take off their boots and wring out their socks, we want the public to know what it is for.

ANOTHER SUGGESTION.

WE were surprised and grieved to see, on Monday evening, a man in the dress circle at the performance of Hazel Kirke at Blackburn's Grand Opera House, who had communed with the maddening bowl till he was considerably elated. When Pitticus made a good hit, or Hazel struck a moist lead, and everybody wept softly on the carpet, this man furnished a war-whoop that not only annoyed the audience, but seemed also to break up the actors a little. Later, he got more quiet, and at last went to sleep and slid out of his chair on the floor. It is such little episodes as these that make strangers dissatisfied with the glorious west. When you go to see something touchful on the stage, you do not care to have your finer feelings ruffled by the yells of a man who has got a corner on delirium tremens.

It is also humiliating to our citizens to be pulled up off the floor by the coat-collar and steered out the door by a policeman.

We hope that as progress is more plainly visible in Wyoming, and as we get more and more refined, such things will be of less and less frequent occurrence, till a man can go to see a theatrical performance with just as much comfort as he would in New York and other eastern towns.

Another point while we are discussing the performance of Hazel Kirke. There were some present on Monday night, sitting hack in the third balcony, who need a theatrical guide to aid them in discovering which are the places to weep and which to gurgle.

It was a little embarrassing to Miss Ellsler to make a grand dramatic hit that was supposed to yank loose a freshet of woe, to be greeted with a snort of demoniac laughter from the rear of the grand opera house.

It seemed to unnerve her and surprise her, but she kept her balance and her head. When death and ruin, and shame and dishonor, were pictured in their tragic horror, the wild, unfettered humorist of a crude civilization fairly yelled with delight. He thought that the tomb and such things were intended to be synonymous with the minstrel show and the circus. He thought that old Dunstan Kirke was there with his sightless eyes to give Laramie the grandest, riproaringest tempest of mirth that she had ever experienced. That is why we say that we will never have a successful performance in the theatrical line, till some of this class are provided with laugh-and-cry guide books.

PISCATORIAL AND EDITORIAL

A CORRESPONDENT of the New York *Post* says that the codfish frequents "the table lands of the sea." The codfish, no doubt, does this to secure as nearly as possible a dry, bracing atmosphere. This pure air of the submarine table lands gives to the codfish that breadth of chest and depth of lungs which we have always noticed.

The glad, free smile of the codfish is largely attributed to the exhilaration of this oceanic altitoodleum.

The correspondent further says, that "the cod subsists largely on the sea cherry." Those who have not had the pleasure of seeing the codfish climb the sea cherry tree in search of food, or clubbing the fruit from the heavily-laden branches with chunks of coral, have missed a very fine sight.

The codfish, when at home rambling through the submarine forests, does not wear his vest unbuttoned, as he does while loafing around the grocery stores of the United States.

ANOTHER FEATHERED SONGSTER

A FORT STEELE taxidermist has presented this office with a stuffed bird of prey about nine feet high, which we have put up in *The Boomerang* office, and hereby return thanks for. It is a kind of a cross between a dodo and a meander-up-the-creek. Its neck is long, like the right of way to a railway, and its legs need some sawdust to make them look healthy. Those who subscribe for the paper, can look at this great work of art free.

This bird is noted for its brief and horizontal alimentary canal. It has no devious digestive arrangements, but contents itself with an economical and unostentatious trunk-line of digestion so simple that any child can understand it. He (or she, as the case may be) in his (or her) stocking feet can easily look over into next fall, and when standing in our office, peers down at us from over the stove-pipe in a reproachful way that fills us with remorse.

We have labeled it "The Democrat Wading Up Salt Creek" and filed it away near the skull of an Indian that we killed years ago when we got mad and wiped out a whole tribe. The geological name of this bird we do not at this moment recall, but it is one of those sorrowful-looking fowls that stick their legs out behind when they fly, and are not good for food.

Parties wishing to see the bird, and subscribe for the *Home Journal* can obtain an audience by kicking three times on the last hall door on the left and throwing two dollars through the transom.

ABOUT THE OSTRICH.

THERE is some prospect of ostrich farming developing into quite an industry in the southwest, and it will sometime be a cold day when the simple-minded rustic of that region will not have ostrich on toast if he wants it. Ostrich farming, however, will always have its drawbacks. The hen ostrich is not a good layer as a rule, only laying two eggs per annum, which, being about the size of a porcelain wash bowl, make her so proud that she takes the balance of the year for the purpose of convalescing.

The ostrich is chiefly valuable for the plumage which he wears, and which, when introduced into the world of commerce, makes the husband almost wish that he were dead.

Probably the ostrich will not come into general use as an article of food, few people caring for it, as the meat is coarse, and the gizzard full of old hardware, and relics of wrecked trains and old irons left where there has been a fire.

Carving the ostrich is not so difficult as carving the quail, because the joints are larger and one can find them with less trouble. Still, the bird takes up a great deal of room at the table, and the best circles are not using them.

The ostrich does not set She don't have time. She does not squat down over something and insist on hatching it out if it takes all summer, but she just lays a couple of porcelain cuspidors in the hot sand when she feels like it, and then goes away to the seaside to quiet her shattered nerves.

TOO MUCH GOD AND NO FLOUR.

OLD CHIEF POCOTELLO, now at the Fort Hall agency, in answer to an inquiry relative to the true Christian character of a former Indian agent at that place, gave in very terse language the most accurate description of a hypocrite that was ever given to the public. "Ugh! Too much God and no flour."

WE ARE GETTING CYNICAL.

IT begins to look now as though Major F. G. Wilson, who stopped here a short time last week and week before, might be a gentleman in disguise. He has done several things since he left here, that look to a man up a tree like something irregular and peculiar. The major has not only prevaricated, but he has done so in such a way as to beat his friends and to make them yearn for his person in order that they may kick him over into the inky night of space. He has represented himself as confidential adviser and literary tourist of several prominent New York, Chicago, Omaha and Tie Siding dailies, and had such good documents to show in proof of his identity in that capacity that he has received many courtesies which, as an ordinary American dead-beat, he might have experienced great difficulty in securing. We simply state this in order to put our esteemed contemporaries on their guard, so that they will not let him spit in their overshoes and enjoy himself as he did here. He wears a white hat on his head and a crooked tooth in the piazza of his mouth. This pearly fang he uses to masticate and reduce little delicate irregular fragments of plug tobacco, which he borrows of people who have time to listen to the silvery tinkle of his bazoo.

When last seen he was headed west, and will probably strike Eureka, Nevada, in a week or two. His mission seems to be mainly to make people feel a goneness in their exchequer, and to distribute tobacco dados over the office stoves of our great land. He is a man who writes long letters to the New York *Herald* that are never printed. His freshly blown nose is red, but his newspaper articles are not. He claims to represent the Mutual Reserve Fund Life Association lately, too. The company represents the Insurance and he attends to the Mutual Reserve Fund. He has mutually reserved all the funds he could get hold of since he struck the west, besides mutually reserving enough strong drink to eat a hole through the Ames monument.

Such men as Major Wilson make us suspicious of humanity, and very likely the next man who comes along here and represents that he is a great man, and wants five dollars on his well-rounded figure and fair fame will have to be identified. We have helped forty or fifty such men to make a bridal tour of Wyoming and now we are going to saw off and quit. When a great journalist comes into this office again with an internal revenue tax on his breath and nineteen dollars back on his baggage, we will probably pick up a fifty pound chunk of North Park quartz and spread his intellectual faculties around this building till it looks like the Custer massacre.

ASK US SOMETHING DIFFICULT.

W HAT becomes of our bodies?" asks a soft eyed scientist, and we answer in stentorian tones, that they get inside of a red flannel undershirt as the maple turns to crimson and the sassafras to gold. Ask us something difficult, ethereal being, if you want to see us get up and claw for our library of public documents.

A MINING EXPERIMENT.

A MILD-EYED youth, wearing a dessert-spoon hat and polka-dot socks, went into Middle Park the other day and claimed to be a mining expert. The boys inveigled him into driving a stick of giant powder into a drill-hole at the bottom of a shaft with an old axe, and now they are trying to get him out of the ground with ammonia and a tooth-brush.

A NEW INDUSTRY.

THE want column of the Chicago *News* for October 10th has the following: "Twelve frightful examples' wanted, to travel with Scott Marble's new drama and appear in the realistic bar-room scene of the 'Drunkard's Daughter.' Arthur G. Cambridge, dramatic agent, 75 South Clark street."

This throws open a field of usefulness to a class of men who hitherto have seen no prospect whatever for the future. It brings within the reach of such men a business which, requiring no capital, still gives the actor much time to do as he chooses. Beauty often wins for itself a place in the great theatrical world, but it is rare that the tomato nose and the watery eye secure a salary for their proprietors. Business must be picking up when the wiggly legs and danger-signal nose will bring so much per week and railroad fare. Perhaps prohibition has got the "frightful example" business down to where it commands the notice of the world because of its seldom condition.

THE MIMIC STAGE.

AT the performance of "The Phoenix" here, the other night, there was a very affecting place where the play is transferred very quickly from a street scene to the elegant apartments of Mr. Blackburn, the heavy villain. The street scene had to be raised out of the way, and the effect of the transition was somewhat marred by the reluctance of the scenery in rolling up out of the way. It got about half way up, and stopped there in an undecided manner, which annoyed the heavy villain a good deal. He started to make some blood-curdling remarks about Mr. Bludsoe, and had got pretty well warmed up when the scenery came down with a bang on the stage. The artist who pulls up the curtain and fills the hall lamps, then pulled the scene up so as to show the villain's feet for fifteen or twenty minutes, but he couldn't get it any farther. It seemed that the clothes line, by which the elaborate scenery is operated, got tangled up some way, and this caused the delay. After that another effort was made, and this time the street scene rolled up to about the third story of a brick hotel shown in the foreground, and stopped there, while the clarionet and first violin continued a kind of sad tremulo. Then a dark hand, with a wart on one finger and an oriental dollar store ring on another, came out from behind the wings and began to wind the clothes-line carefully around the pole at the foot of the scene. The villain then proceeded with his soliloquy, while the street scene hung by one corner in such a way as to make a large warehouse on the corner of the street stand at an angle of about forty-five degrees.

Laramie will never feel perfectly happy until these little hitches are dispensed with. Supposing that at some place in the play, where the heroine is speaking soft and low to her lover and the proper moment has arrived for her to pillow her sunny head upon his bosom, that street scene should fetch loose, and come down with such momentum as to knock the lovers over into the arms of the bass-viol player. Or suppose that in some death-bed act this same scene, loaded with a telegraph pole at the bottom, should settle down all at once in such a way as to leave the death-bed out on the corner of Monroe and Clark streets, in front of a candy store.

Modern stage mechanism has now reached such a degree of perfection that the stage carpenter does not go up on a step ladder, in the middle of a play, and nail the corner of a scene to a stick of 2x4 scantling, while a duel is going on near the step ladder. In all the larger theatres and opera houses, now, they are not doing that way.

Of course little incidents occur, however, even on the best stages, and where the whole thing works all right. For instance, the other day, a young actor, who was kneeling to a beautiful heiress down east, got a little too far front, and some scenery, which was to come together in the middle of the stage to pianissimo music, shut him outside and divided the tableau in two, leaving the young actor apparently kneeling at the foot of a street lamp, as though he might be hunting for a half a dollar that he had just dropped on the sidewalk.

There was a play in New York, not long ago, in which there was a kind of military parade introduced, and the leader of a file of soldiers had his instructions to march three times around the stage to martial music, and then file off at the left, the whole column, of course, following him. After marching once around, the stage manager was surprised to see the leader deliberately wheel, and walk off the stage, at the left, with the whole battalion following at his heels. The manager went to him and abused him shamefully for his haste, and told him he had a mind to discharge him; but the talented hack driver, who thus acted as the military leader, and who had over-played himself by marching off the stage ahead of time, said:

"Well, confound it, you can discharge me if you want to, but what was a man to do? Would you have me march around three times when my military pants were coming off, and I knew it? Military pride, pomp, parade, and circumstance, are all right; but it can be overdone. A military squadron, detachment, or whatever it is, can make more of a parade, under certain circumstances, than is advertised. I didn't want to give people more show than they paid for, and I ask you to put yourself in my place. When a man is paid three dollars a week to play a Roman soldier, would you have him play the Greek slave? No, sir; I guess I know what I'm hired to play, and I'm going to play it. When you want me to play Adam in the Garden of Eden, just give me my fig leaf and salary enough to make it interesting, and I will try and properly interpret the character for you, or refund the money at the door."

THE MIMIC STAGE.

Complicated scenic effects.

DECLINE OF AMERICAN HUMOR.

D EAR, mellow-voiced, starry-eyed reader, did you ever see something about "the decline of American humor?" Well, we got a gob of American humor, yesterday, written by a yahoo with pale pink hair, which was entitled "Marriage in Mormondom on the Tontine Plan." Well, we declined it. Decline of American humor. *Sabe?*

CHICAGO CUSTOM HOUSE.

THE Chicago custom house and post office, built from designs by Oscar Wild, and other delirum tremens artists, is getting wiggly, and bids fair to some day fall down and scrunch about 500 United States employes into the great billowy sea of the eternal hence. It is a sick looking structure, with little gothic warts on top, and red window sashes, and little half-grown smoke houses sprouting out of it in different places. It is grand, gloomy and peculiar, and looks as though it might be cursed with an inward pain.

FOREIGN OPINION.

WE are indebted to Fred J. Prouting, correspondent of the foreign and British newspaper press, for a copy of the London *Daily* of the 9th inst., containing the following editorial notice:

"If ever celebrity were attained unexpectedly, most assuredly it was that thrust upon Bill Nye by Truthful James. It is just possible, however, that the innumerable readers of Mr. Bret Harte's 'Heathen Chinee' may have imagined Bill Nye and Ah Sin to be purely mythical personages. So far as the former is concerned, any such conclusion now appears to have been erroneous. Bill Nye is no more a phantom than any other journalist, although the name of the organ which he 'runs' savors more of fiction than of fact. But there is no doubt about the matter, for the Washington correspondent of the New York *Tribune* telegraphed on the 29th instant, that Bill Nye had accepted a post under the government. He has lately been domiciled in Laramie City, Wyoming territory, and is editor of The Daily Boomerang. In reference to Acting-Postmaster-Gen. Hatton's appointment of him as postmaster at Laramie City, the opponent of Ah Sin writes an extremely humorous letter, 'extending' his thanks, and advising his chief of his opinion that his 'appointment is a triumph of eternal truth over error and wrong.' Nye continues: 'It is one of the epochs, I may say, in the nation's onward march toward political purity and perfection. I don't know when I have noticed any stride in the affairs of state which has so thoroughly impressed me with its wisdom.' In this quiet strain of banter, Bill Nye continues to the end of his letter, which suggests the opinion that whatever the official qualifications of the new postmaster may be, the inhabitants of Laramie City must have a very readable newspaper in The Daily Boomerang."

While thanking our London contemporary for its gentle and harmless remarks, we desire to correct an erroneous impression that the seems to have as to our general style: The British press has in some way arrived at the conclusion that the editor of this fashion-guide and mental lighthouse on the rocky shores of time (terms cash), is a party with wild tangled hair, and an like a tongue of flame.

That is not the case, and therefore our English co-worker in the great field of journalism is, no doubt, laboring under a popular misapprehension. Could the editor of the *News* look in upon us as we pull down tome after tome of forgotten lore in our study; or, with a glad smile, glance hurriedly over the postal card in transit through our postoffice, he would see, not as he supposes, a wild and cruel slayer of his fellow men, but a thoughtful, scholarly and choice fragment of modern architecture, with lines of care about the firmly chiseled mouth, and with the subdued and chastened air of a man who has run for the legislature and failed to get there, Eli.

The London *News* is an older paper than ours, and we therefore recognize the value of its kind notice. *The Boomerang* is a young paper, and has therefore only begun fairly to do much damage as a national misfortune, but the time is not far distant, when, from Greenland's icy mountains to India's coral strand, we propose to search out suffering humanity and make death easier and more desirable, by introducing this choice malady.

Regarding the postoffice, we wish to state that we shall aim to make it a great financial success, and furnish mail at all times to all who desire it, whether they have any or not. We shall be pretty busy, of course, attending to the office during the day, and writing scathing editorials during the night, but we will try to snatch a moment now and then to write a few letters for those who have been inquiring sadly and hopelessly for letters during the past ten years. It is, indeed, a dark and dreary world to the man who has looked in at the same general delivery window nine times a day for ten years, and yet never received a letter, nor even a confidential postal card from a commercial man, stating that on the 5th of the following month he would strike the town with a new and attractive line of samples.

We should early learn to find put such suffering as that, and if we are in the postoffice department we may be the means of much good by putting new envelopes on our own dunning letters and mailing them to the suffering and distressed. Let us, in our abundance, remember those who have not been dunned for many a weary year. It will do them good, and we will not feel the loss.

THEY HAVE CURBED THEIR WOE.

T HEY say that Brigham Young's grave is looking as bare and desolate as a boulevard now. At first, while her grief was fresh, his widow used to march out there five abreast, and just naturally deluge the grave with scalding tears, and at that time the green grass grew luxuriantly, and the pig-weed waved in the soft summer air; but as she learned to control her emotions, the humidity of the atmosphere disappeared, and grief's grand irrigation failed to give down. We should learn from this that the man who flatters himself that in marrying a whole precinct during life, he is piling up for the future a large invoice of ungovernable woe, is liable to get left. The prophet's tomb looks to-day like a deserted buffalo wallow, while his widow has dried her tears, and is trying to make a mash on the Utah commission. Such is life in the far west, and such the fitting resting place of a red-headed old galvanized prophet, who marries a squint-eyed fly-up-the-creek, and afterward gets a special revelation requiring him to marry a female mass-meeting. Let us be thankful for what we have, instead of yearning for a great wealth of wife. Then the life insurance will not have to be scattered so, and our friends will be spared the humiliating spectacle of a bereft and sorrowing herd of widow, turned loose by the cold hand of death to monkey o'er our tomb.

HUNG BY REQUEST.

THIS county has had two hemp carnivals during the past few weeks, and it begins to look like old times again. In each case the murder was unprovoked, and the victim a quiet gentleman. That is why there was a popular feeling against the murderer, and a spontaneous ropestretching benefit as a result. While we deplore the existence of a state of affairs that would warrant these little expressions of feeling, we cannot come right out and condemn the exercises which followed.

The more we read the political record of the candidate for office, as set forth in opposing journals, the more we feel that there are already few enough good men in this country, so that we do not care to spare any of them. If, therefore, the mischievous bad man is permitted to thin them out this way, the day is not distant when we won't have good men enough to run the newspapers, to say nothing of other avocations.

We know that eastern people will speak of us as a ferocious tribe on the Wyoming reservation, but we desire to call the attention of our more law-abiding brethren to the fact that there has been in the past year a lynching in almost every state in the Union, to say nothing of several hundred cases where there should have been. Do you suppose Wyoming young ladies would consent to play the waltz known as "Under the Elms," composed by Walter Malley, if Walter had been as frolicsome here as he was down on the Atlantic coast? Scarcely. We may be the creatures of impulse here, but not that kind of impulse.

Minneapolis hung a man during the past year, and so did Bloomington and other high-toned towns, and shall we, because we are poor and lonely, be denied this poor boon? We hope not. Because we have left the East and moved out here to make some money and build up a new country, shall we be refused the privileges we would have enjoyed if we had remained in the states. We trow not.

A telegraph pole with a remains hanging on it is not a cheerful sight, but it has a tendency to annoy and mentally disturb those who contemplate the violent death of some good man. It unnerves the brave assassin and makes him restless and apprehensive. Death is always depressing, but it is doubly so when it has that purple and suffocated appearance which is noticeable in the features of the early fall fruit of the telegraph pole. Lately, we will state, however, the telegraph pole has fallen into disfavor, and is not much used, owing to a rumor which gained circulation some time ago, to the effect that Jay Gould intended to charge the vigilance committee rent.

A COLORED GREEK SLATE.

A NUDE colored woman, as wild as a gorilla, startling the people of the Marvel section of Missouri. She has been seen several times, and the last time threw a young lady, who was horseback riding, into hysteria, and with a grunt—not unlike that of a wild hog—jumped up and ran into the forest. At the time of her discovery she was burrowing into the side of the road, catching and eating crawfish, which she ate claws, hide and all. She is very black, and foams at the mouth when angry, like a wild animal at bay. She is probably a colored Greek slave in search of an umbrella and the remainder of her wardrobe. Still, she may be a brunette society belle, who went in swimming where a mud-turtle caught her by the pink toe, and the nervous shock has unsettled her mind.

THE MELVILLES.

AN exchange says that Mrs. Melville has become deranged through excess of joy over the unexpected return of her husband. Another one says that it is thought that Lieutenant Melville is off his basement as a result of exposure to the vigorous and bracing air of the north pole. Still another says that Mr. Melville was always mean and hateful toward his wife, and that when he was at home, she had to do her own washing and wind the clock herself. From the different stories now floating about relative to the Melville family, we are led to believe that he is a kind and considerate husband, pleasant and good-natured toward his wife—while asleep; and that she is a kind, beautiful and accomplished wife—when she is sober. How many of our best wives are falling victims to the alcoholic habit recently! How sad to think that, as husbands, we will soon be left to wait and watch and vigil through the long, weary night for that one to return who promised us on the nuptial day that she would protect and love us. Ah, what a silent, but seductive foe to the husband is rum! How it creeps into the home circle and snatches the wife in the full blush and bloom of womanhood, while the pale, sad-eyed husband sits at the sewing machine and barely makes enough to keep the little ones from want.

No one can fully realize, but he who has been there, so to speak, the terrible shock that Mr. Melville received on the first evening that his wife came staggering home. No one can tell how the pain froze his throbbing gizzard, or how he shuddered in the darkness, and filled the pillow-sham full of sobs when he first knew that she had got it up her nose. Ah, what a picture of woe we see before us. There in the solemn night, robed in? long, plainly constructed garment of pure white, buttoned at the throat in a negligent manner, stands Mr. Melville with his bare, tall brow glistening in the flickering rays of a kerosene lamp, which he holds in his hand, while on the front porch stands the wife who a few years ago promised to defend and protect him. She is a little unsteady on her feet, and her hat is out of plumb. She tries to be facetious, and asks him if that is where Mr. Melville lives. He looks at her coldly and says it is, but unfortunately it is not an inebriate's home and refuge for the budge demolisher. Then he bursts into tears, and his sobs shake the entire ranch. But we draw a curtain over the scene.

A year later he may be discovered about two miles southwest of the north pole. Cool, but happy. He is trying to forget his woe. He smells like sperm-oil and looks like a bald-headed sausage, but the woe of drink is forgotten.'

How sad that he has returned and suffered again. What a mistake that he did not remain where, instead of his wife's coolness, he would have had only that of nature to contend against.

MENDING BROKEN NECKS.

THEY have successfully set a boy's broken neck, in Connecticut, and now it looks as though the only way to kill a man is to take him about 200 miles from any physician, and run him through a Hoe Perfecting Press. If this thing continues, they will some day put some electricity into Pharaoh's daughter and engage her as a ballet-dancer, along with other tender pullets of her own age.

ARE YOU A MORMON?

W E are indebted to Elder Wilkins, of Logan, Utah, first-assistant-general-tooly-muck-a-hi Z. C. M. I. and Z. W. of T. U. O. M. and B. company, and president of the cache stake of Zion, constituting last in the quorum of seventies, for the late edition of the Mormon Guide and Hand Book of the Endowment House. It is a very pleasant work to read, and makes the whole endowment scheme as clear to the average mind as though he had been through it personally.

Pictures of the endowment chemiloon and Z. C. M. I. bib are given to show the novice exactly how they appear to the unclothed and unregenerate vision. The convert, it seems, first goes to the desk, on entering, and registers. Then she leaves her every-day clothes in the baggage room and gets a check for them. The next thing on the programme is a bath, called the farewell bath, because it is the last one taken by the endowment victim.

The convert is then anointed with machine oil from a cow's horn, after which she is named something, supposed to be the celestial cognomen. Then comes the endowment robe, which is a combination arrangement that don't look pretty. After that, the apprentice to polygamy goes into an impromptu garden of Eden, where the apple business is gone through with. A thick-necked path-master from Logan takes the character of Adam, and a pale-haired livery stable keeper from Salt Lake acts as the ruler of the universe. This is not making light of a sacred subject. It is just the simple, plain, horrible truth.

The creation of the world is thus gone through with by these blatant priests of Latter Day bogus sanctity, and the exercises are continued after this fashion through all their disgusting details. We have no time or inclination to enlarge upon them. Truth is sometimes nauseating, especially while discussing the Mormon problem.

If Brigham Young had lived, he would have helped out his church by a revelation that would have knocked the daylights out of polygamy; but as it is now, John Taylor, with his characteristic stubborness, will not attend to it, his revelation machine being somewhat out of whack, as Oscar Wilde would say, so that the anointing with the so-called sanctified lubricant will continue till the United States sits down on the whole grand farce.

ELDER DON MIGUEL CONNUBIALSON, AS ADAM, BY NYE.

CAUTION.

A MAN is going about the streets of Laramie claiming to be John the Baptist. He has light hair and chin whiskers, is stout built and looks like a farmer. We desire to warn those of our readers who may be inclined to trust him, that he is not what he purports to be. We have taken great pains to look the matter up, and find, as a result of our research, that John the Baptist is dead.

A BLOW TO THE GOVERNMENT.

At the October term of the district court we shall resign the office of United States Commissioner for this judicial district, an office which we have held so long, and with such great credit to ourself. Fearing that in the hurry and rush of other business our contemporaries might overlook the matter, we have consented to mention, briefly, the fact that at the opening of court, Judge Blair will be called upon to accept the resignation of one of our most tried and true officials, who has for so long held up this corner of the great national fabric.

It has been our solemn duty to examine the greaser who sold liquor to our red brother, and filled him up with the deadly juice of the sour-mash tree. It has devolved upon us to singe the soft-eyed lad who stole baled hay from the reservation, and it has also been our glorious privilege to examine, in a preliminary manner, the absent-minded party who gathered unto himself the U. S. mule.

We have attempted to resign before, but failed. One reason was, that it was a novel proceeding in Wyoming, and no one seemed to know how to go to work at it. No one had ever resigned before, and the matter had to be hunted up and the law thoroughly understood.

The office is one of great profit, as we have said before. It brings wealth into the coffers of the U. S. Commissioner in a way that is well calculated to turn the head of most people. We have, however, succeeded in controlling ourself, and have so far suppressed that beastly pride which wealth engenders. With a salary of $7.25 per annum, and lead pencils, we have-steadily refused to go to Europe, preferring rather to plod along here in the wild west, although we may never see the beauties of a foreign shore.

Official duty was at all times weighing upon our mind like a leaden load. Oft in the stilly night we have been wakened by the oppressing thought that, perhaps at that moment, on some distant reservation, some pale-faced villain might be selling valley-tan to the gentle, untutored Indian brave, and it has tortured us and robbed us of slumber and joy. Now it is a relief to know that very soon we shall be free from this great responsibility. If an Indian gets drunk on the reservation, or a time-honored government mule is stolen, we shall not be expected to get up in the night and administer swift and terrible justice to the offender. Old-man-with-a-torpid-liver can go as drunk as he pleases on the reservation. It does not come under our jurisdiction any more. We can sleep now nights while some other man peels his coat, and acts as the United States nemesis for this diocese.

Sometime during the ensuing week we will turn over the lead pencil and the blotting paper of the office to our successor. We leave the Indian temperance movement in his hands. The United States mule, kleptomaniac also, we leave with him. With a clear conscience and an unliquidated claim against the government for $9.55, the earnings of the past two years, we turn over the office, knowing that although we have sacrificed our health, we have never evaded our duty, no matter how dangerous or disagreeable.

Yet we do not ask for any gold-headed cane as a mark of esteem on the part of the government. We have a watch that does very well for us, so that a testimonial consisting of a gold watch, costing $250, would be unnecessary. Any little trinket of that kind would, of course, show how ready the department of justice is to appreciate the work of an efficient officer, but we do not look for it, nor ask it. A thoroughly fumigated and disinfected conscience is all we want. That is enough for us. Do not call out the band. Just let us retire from the office quietly and unostentatiously. As regards the United States Commissionership, we retire to private life. In the bosom of our family we will forget the turbulent voyage of official life through which we have passed, and as we monkey with the children around our hearthstone, we will shut our eyes to the official suffering that is going on on all around us.

POISONS AND THEIR ANECDOTES.

AN amateur scientist sends us a long article written with a purple pencil on both sides of twelve sheets of legal cap, and entitled "Poisons and Their Anecdotes."

Will the soft-eyed mullet-head please call and get it, also a lick over the eye with a hot stove leg, and greatly oblige the weary throbbing brain that, moulds the scientific course of this paper?

CORRESPONDENCE.

CHEYENNE, SEPTEMBER 6, 1882.

THE party, consisting of Governor Hale and wife, Secretary Morgan and wife, President Slack, of the "Wyoming Press Association, and wife, Mr. Baird and myself, started out of Laramie, about 8:30 last evening, and excurted along over the hill with some hesitation, arriving here this morning at four o'clock. The engine at first slipped an eccentric on Dale Creek bridge, and we remained there some time, delayed but happy. Then, as the night wore away and the gray dawn came down over the broad and mellow sweep of plain to the eastward, an engine ahead of us on a freight train blew off her monkey-wrench, and we were delayed in the neighborhood of Hazzard several more hours. Hazzard is a thriving town on the eastern slope of the mountains, with glorious possibilities for a town site. With gas and waterworks and a city debt of $200,000, Hazzard will some day attract notice from the civilized world. If her vast deposits of sand and alkali could be brought to the notice of capital, Hazzard would some day take rank with such cities as Wilcox and Tie City.

Still we had a good deal of fun. We heard that Whitelaw Reid, of the New York was on board, and we sent the porter into the other car after him. Mr. Reid did not behave as we thought he would at first. We had presumed that he was cold and distant in his manners, but he is not. As soon as the first embarrassment of meeting us was over, he sailed right in and did all the talking himself, just as any cultivated gentleman would. He told us all about New York politics and how he was fighting the machine, at the same time, however, casually dropping a remark or two that led us to conclude that it was only one machine that didn't want another one to win. He is a tall, rather fine-looking man, with a Grecian nose and long, dark hair, which he does up in tin foil at night. I told him that I was grieved to know that his hired man had, inadvertently no doubt, referred to me in a manner that gave the American people an idea that I was a good deal bigger man than I really was. I asked him whether he wanted to apologize then and there or be thrown over Dale Creek bridge into the rip-snorting torrent below.

He said he didn't believe that such a remark had been made, but if it had he would go home and kill the man who wrote it, if that would poultice up my wounded heart. I said it would. If he would just mail me the remains of the man who made the remark, not necessarily for publication, but as a guarantee of good faith, it would be all right.

We talked all night, and incurred the everlasting displeasure of a fat man from San Francisco, who told the porter he wanted his money back because he hadn't slept any all night. He seemed mad because we were having a little harmless conversation among ourselves, and when the clock in the steeple struck four he rolled over in his berth, gave a large groan and then got up and dressed. Some people are so morbidly nervous that they cannot sleep on a train, and they naturally get cross and say ungentlemanly things. This man said some things while he was dressing and buttoning his suspenders, that made my blood run cold. A man who has no better control of his temper than that, ought not to travel at all. He just simply makes a North American side-show of himself.

Cheyenne is very greatly improved since I was here last. The building up of the corner opposite the Inter Ocean hotel has added greatly to the attractiveness of the Magic City, and other work is being done which enhances the beauty of the city very much. F. E. Warren is one of the most enterprising and thoroughly vigorous western business men I ever knew. He is an anomaly, I might say. When I say he is an anomaly, I do not mean to reflect upon him in any way, though I do not know the meaning of the word. I simply mean that he is the chief grand rustle of a very rustling city.

WHAT THE DEMOCRATIC PARTY NEEDS.

THE candidate for county commissioner, on the Democratic ticket, of Sweetwater county, keeps a drug store, and when a little girl burned her arm against the cook stove, and her father went after a package of Russia salve, the genial Bourbon gave her a box of "Rough on Rats." What the Democratic party needs, is not so much a new platform, but a carload of assorted brains that some female seminary had left over.

A LETTER FROM LEADVILLE.

LEADVILLE, COLORADO, SEPT. 10.

THIS morning we rose at 4:30, and rode from Buena Vista to Leadville, arriving at the Clarendon for breakfast. Our party has been reduced in one way and another until there are only eight here to-day. Secretary Morgan and family remained at Buena Vista on account of the illness of Misa Lillie Morgan, who suffers severely from sea-sickness on the mountain railroads.

One thing I have not mentioned, and an incident certainly worthy of note, was the sudden decision of our president, E. A. Slack, on Friday, to remain at a little station on the South Parle road, above Como, while the party continued on to Buena Vista. Mr. Slack is a man of iron will and sudden impulses, as all who know him are aware. He got in a car at the station referred to, and under the impression that it belonged to our train, remained in it till he got impatient about something, and asked a man who came in with a broom, why we were making such a stop at that station. The man said that this car had been side-tracked, and the train had gone sometime ago.

Then Mr. Slack made the rash remark that he would remain there until the next train. He acts readily in an emergency, and he saw at a glance that the best thing that he could do would be to just stay there, and examine the country until he could get the next train. He telegraphed us that the fare was so high on our train that he would see if he couldn't get better rates on the following day. In the meantime, he struck Superintendent Egbert's special car, and rode around over the country till morning, while our party took in Buena Vista. The city is but two years old, but very thriving, and has 2,500 to 3,000 population. At the depot we were met by Agent Smith, of the South Park road, who had secured rooms for us at the Grand Park hotel. He had also arranged for carriages to take us out to Cottonwood Hot Springs, about six miles up Cottonwood creek, where we took supper. We found a first-class sixty-four room hotel there, with hot baths, and everything comfortable and neat. The proprietors are Messrs. Stafford and Hartenstein—the latter having been a medical student under Dr. Agnew. After a good-supper we returned to Buena Vista, where the home military company, under Captain Johnson, led by the Buena Yista band, serenaded us. I responded in a brief but telling speech, which I would give here if I had not forgotten what it was. Some of the other members of the party wanted to make the speech, but I said no, it would not be right. I was representing the president, Mr. Slack, and wearing his overcoat, and therefore it would devolve on me to make the grand opening remarks. It was the greatest effort of my life, and town lots in Buena Vista depreciated fifty per cent.

We found A. D. Butler, formerly of Cheyenne, now at Buena Vista, also Tom Campbell, well known to Laramie people, doing well at the new city, and a prospective member of the Colorado legislature. George Marion, formerly of Laramie, is also at Buena Vista, engaged in the retail bridge trade. We also met Messrs. Leonard, of the and Kennedy, of the *Herald*, who treated us the whitest kind. Mr. Leonard and wife went with us yesterday over to Gunnison City. Billy Butler, formerly of Laramie, is now at Buena Vista, successfully engaged in mining.

Yesterday we put in the most happy day of the entire trip. Under the very kind and thoughtful guidance of Superintendent E. Wilbur, of the Gunnison division of the South Park road, we went over the mountain to Gunnison and through the wonderful Alpine tunnel, the highest railroad point in the United States, and with its approaches 2,600 feet long. When you pass through the tunnel the brakeman makes you close your window and take in your head. He does this for two reasons: first, you can't see anything if you look out, and secondly, the company don't like to hire an extra man to go through the tunnel twice a day and wipe the remains of tourists off the walls.

The newsboy told me that a tourist from Philadelphia once tried to wipe his nose on the Alpine tunnel, while the train was in motion, and when they got through into daylight, and his companions told him to take in his head, he couldn't do it—because it was half a mile behind examining the formation of the tunnel. Later, it was found that the man was dead. The passengers said that they noticed a kind of crunching noise while going through the tunnel that sounded like the smashing of false teeth, but they paid no attention to it.

Mr. Wilbur afterward told me that there had never been a passenger killed on the road, so I may have been misled by this newsboy. Still, he didn't look like a boy who would trifle with a man's feelings in that way.

However, I will leave the remainder of the Gunnison trip for another letter, as this is already too long.

TABLE MANNERS OF CHILDREN.

Y OUNG children who have to wait till older people have eaten all there is in the house, should not open the dining-room door during the meal and ask the host if he is going to eat all day. It makes the company feel ill at ease, and lays up wrath in the parents' heart.

Children should not appear displeased with the regular courses at dinner, and then fill up on pie. Eat the less expensive food first, and then organize a picnic in the preserves afterward.

Do not close out the last of your soup by taking the plate in your mouth and pouring the liquid down your childish neck. You might spill it on your bosom, and it enlarges and distorts the mouth unnecessarily.

When asked what part of the fowl you prefer, do not say you will take the part that goes over the fence last. This remark is very humorous, but the rising generation ought to originate some new table jokes that will be worthy of the age in which we live.

Children should early learn the use of the fork, and how to handle it. This knowledge can be acquired by allowing them to pry up the carpet tacks with this instrument, and other little exercises, such as the parent mind may suggest.

The child should be taught at once not to wave his bread around over the table, while in conversation, or to fill his mouth full of potatoes, and then converse in a rich tone of voice with some one out in the yard. He might get his dinner down his trochea and cause his parents great anxiety.

In picking up a plate or saucer filled with soup or with moist food, the child should be taught not to parboil his thumb in the contents of the dish, and to avoid swallowing soup bones or other indigestible debris.

Toothpicks are generally the last course, and children should not be permitted to pick their teeth and kick the table through the other exercises. While grace is being said at table, children should know that it is a breach of good breeding to smouge fruit cake just because their parents' heads are bowed down, and their attention for the moment turned in another direction. Children ought not to be permitted to find fault with the dinner, or fool with the cat while they are eating. Boys should, before going to the table, empty all the frogs and grasshoppers out of their pockets, or those insects might crawl out during the festivities, and jump into the gravy.

If a fly wades into your jelly up to his gambrels, do not mash him with your spoon before all the guests, as death is at all times depressing to those who are at dinner, and retards digestion. Take the fly out carefully, with what naturally adheres to his person, and wipe him on the table cloth. It will demonstrate your perfect command of yourself, and afford much amusement for the company. Do not stand up in your chair and try to spear a roll with your fork. It is not good manners to do so, and you might slip and bust your crust, by so doing. Say "thank you," and "much obliged," and "beg pardon," wherever you can work in these remarks, as it throws people off their guard, and gives you an opportunity to get in your work on the pastry and other bric-a-brac near you at the time.

WHAT IT MEANT.

WHEN Billy Boot was a little boy, he was of a philosophical and investigating turn of mind, and wanted to know almost everything. He also desired to know it immediately. He could not wait for time to develop his intellect, but he crowded things and wore out the patience of his father, a learned savant, who was president of a livery stable in Chicago.

One day Billy ran across the grand hailing sign, which is generally represented as a tapeworm in the beak of the American eagle, on which is inscribed "E Pluribus Unum." Billy, of course, asked his father what "E Pluribus Unum" meant. He wanted to gather in all the knowledge he could, so that when he came out west he could associate with some of our best men.

"I admire your strong appetite for knowledge, Billy," said Mr. Root; "you have a morbid craving for cold hunks of ancient history and cyclopedia that does my soul good; and I am glad, too, that you come to your father to get accurate data for your collection. That is right. Your father will always lay aside his work at any time and gorge your young mind with knowledge that will be as useful to you as a farrow cow. 'E Pluri-bus Unum' is an old Greek inscription that has been handed down from generation to generation, preserved in brine, and signifies that 'the tail goes with the hide.'"

THE MEANING OF "E PLURIBUS UNUM,"

Our Great National Motto.

VOTERS IN UTAH.

THIS is the form of the oath required of voters in Utah under the new law:

Territory of Utah,
County of Salt Lake. } ss.

I — — — — — — being first duly sworn (or affirmed), depose and say that I am over twenty-one years of age, and have resided in the territory of Utah for six months, and in the precinct of — — — — — one month immediately preceding the date thereof, and (if a male) am a native born or naturalized (as the case may be) citizen of the United States and a tax payer in this territory. (Or, if a female) I am native born, or naturalized, or the widow or daughter (as the case may be) of a native born or naturalized citizen of the United States. And I do further solemnly swear (or affirm) that I am not a bigamist or polygamist; that I am not a violater of the laws of the United States prohibiting bigamy or polygamy; that I do not live or cohabit with more than one woman in the marriage relation, nor does any relation exist between me and any woman which has been entered into or continued in violation of said laws of the United States, prohibiting bigamy or polygamy, (and if a woman) that I am not the wife of a polygamist, nor have I entered into any relation with any man in violation of the laws of the United States concerning polygamy or bigamy.

Subscribed and sworn to before me this — — — day of — — — — — —, 1882.

— — — — —

Registration Officer — — — — — Precinct.

It will be seen that at the next election some of the brethren and sisters in Zion will be disfranchised unless they do some pretty tall swearing. This is a terrible state of affairs, and the whole civilized world will feel badly to know that some of our people are going to be left out in the cold, cold world with no voice and no vote just because they have been too zealous in the wedlock business.

Matrimony is a glorious thing, but it can be overdone. A man can become a victim to the nuptial habit just the same as he can the opium habit. It then assumes entire control over him, and he has to be chained up or paralyzed with a club, or he would marry all creation. This law, therefore, is salutary in its operations. It is intended as a gentle check on those who have allowed themselves to become matrimony's maniacs. If we marry one of the daughters of a family, and are happy over it, is that any reason why we should marry the other daughters and the old lady and the colored cook? We think not. It is natural for man to acquire railroads and promissory notes and houses and lands, but he should not undertake to acquire a corner on the wife trade.

Hence we say the law is just and must be permitted to take its course, even though it may disfranchise many of the most prominent pelicans of the Mormon church. Matrimony in Utah has been allowed to run riot, as it were. The cruel and relentless hand of this hydra-headed monster has been laid upon the youngest and the fairest of the Mormon people.

Matrimony has broken out there in a large family in some instances, and has not even spared the widowed and toothless mother. It generally seeks its prey among the youngest and fairest, but in Utah it has not spared even the old and the infirm. Like a cruel epidemic, it has at first raked in the blooming maidens of Mormondom and at last spotted the lantern jawed dregs of foreign female emigration. In one community, this great scourge entered and took all the women under forty-five, and then got into a block where there were nineteen old women who didn't average a tooth apiece, and swept them away like a cyclone.

People who do not know anything of this great evil, can have no knowledge of it. Those who have not investigated this question have certainly failed to look into it. We cannot find out about this question without ascertaining something of it.

INCONGRUITY.

OUR attention has been called recently to an illustration by Hopkins in a work called Forty Liars, in which a miner is represented as sliding down a mountain in a gold pan with a handle on it. Mr. Hopkins, no doubt, labors under a wrong impression of some kind, relative to the gold pan. He seems to consider the gold pan and the frying pan as synonymous. In this he is wrong.

The gold pan is a large low pan without a handle and made of very different metal from a skillet or frying pan.

The artist should study as far as possible to imitate nature and not make a fool of himself. Some artists consider it funny to represent a farmer milking a cow on the wrong side. They also show the same farmer, later on, plowing with a plow that turns the furrow over to the left, another eccentricity of genius. There are many little things like this that the artist should look into more closely so as not to bust up the eternal fitness of things.

We presume that Mr Hopkins would represent a gang of miners working a placer with giant powder and washing out smelting ore in a tin dipper. Its pretty hard, though, for an artist who never saw a mining camp, to sit and watch a New York beer tournament and draw pictures of life in a mining camp, and people ought not to expect too much.

RIDING DOWN A MOUNTAIN.

GUNNISON CITY is one of the peculiarities of a mining boom. It spreads out and slops over the plain like a huge camp meeting, but without shape or beauty.

The plains there are red and sandy; the trees are not nearer than the foot-hills; and the city, which claims 5,000 inhabitants, though 3,000 would, no doubt, be more accurate, is composed of a wide area of ground, with scattering houses that look lonely in the midst of the desolation. Mining in Colorado, this season, has not advanced with the wonderful impetus which characterized it in previous years. Wherever you go, you hear first one reason, and then another, why good mines are not being worked. There is trouble among the stock-holders; a game of freeze out; lack of capital to put in proper machinery, or excessive railroad freights, to pay which virtually paralyzes the reduction of ore owned by men too poor to erect the expensive works necessary to the realization of profit from the mines.

Returning from Gunnison City, now, you rise at a rate of over 200 feet to the mile, zig-zagging up the almost perpendicular mountain, near the summit of which is the Alpine tunnel. As you near the tunnel, there is a perpendicular and sometimes even a jutting wall above you, hundreds of feet at your right, while far below you, on your left, is a yellow streak, which at first you take to be an old mountain trail, but which you soon discover is the circuitous track over which you have just come.

Near here, while the road was being built, a fine span of horses balked on the grade, and like all balky horses, proceeded to back off the road. The owner got out of the wagon, and told them they could keep that thing up if they wanted to, but he could not endorse their policy. They kept backing off until the wagon went over the brink, and then there was a little scratching of loose stones, the kaleidoscope of legs and hoofs, a little rush and rumble, and the world was wealthier by one less balky team. The owner never went down to see where they went to, or how they lit. He was afraid they would not survive their injuries, so he did not go down there. Later, the carrion crows and turkey buzzards indicated where the refractory team had landed; and deep in the mountain gorge the white bones lie amid the wreck of a lumber wagon, as monuments of equine folly.

On Saturday evening we had the pleasure of riding down the dizzy grade from Hancock, a distance of eighteen miles, at which time we descended a mile perpendicularly in a push car, with Superintendent Wilbur as conductor and engineer. A push car is a plain flat-car, about as big as a dining-table, with four wheels, and nothing to propel it but gravity, and nothing to stop it but a sharpened piece of two-by-four scantling. Hancock is near the Alpine tunnel, at the summit of the mountains, about 11,000 feet high. Secretary Morgan, Mrs. Morgan, with their little daughter Gertrude; E. A. Slack, of the *Sun*, Frank Clark, of the *Leader*, Superintendent Wilbur and ourself, constituted the party.

At first everybody was a little nervous with the accumulating velocity of the car, and the yawning abyss below us; but later we got more accustomed to it, and the solemn grandeur of the green pine-covered canons, the lofty snow-covered peaks, apparently so near us; and the rushing, foaming torrent far below us, were all we saw. Like lightning we rounded the sharp curves where the road seemed to hang over instant destruction, and we held our breath as we thought that, like Dutch Charlie and other great men, only a piece of two-by-four scantling stood between us and death.

Again and again the abrupt curve loomed up ahead, and below us, while we flew along the narrow gauge at such a pace that we were almost sure the car would, leave the track before it would round such a point, and each time the two-by-four went down on the drive wheel with a pressure that sent up volumes of blue smoke.

It was a wild, grand ride—so wild and grand in fact that even yet we wake up at night with a start from a dream in which the same party is riding down that canon at lightning speed, and Mr. Wilbur, in a thoughtless moment, has dropped his pine brake overboard!

Shades of Sam Patch, but wouldn't it scatter the average excurter over southern Colorado if such a thing should happen some day! Why, the woods would be full of them, and for years to come, the prospector along Chalk Creek Canon would find pyrites of editorial poverty, and indications of collar buttons, and fragments of Archimedean levers, and other mementoes of the great editorial hegira of 1882.

CORRALED HIM.

LAST May Sheriff Boswell received a postal card from a man up near Fort McKinney, describing a pair of horses that had just been stolen and asking that Mr. Boswell would keep his eye peeled for the thief and arrest him on sight.

Last week the sheriff discovered the identical team with color, brands and everything to correspond. He told the driver that he would have to turn over that team and come along to the bastile. The man stoutly protested his innocence and claimed that he owned the team, but Boswell laughed him to scorn and said he often got such games of talk as that when he arrested horse thieves.

Just as they were going down into the damp corridors, Judge Blair met the criminal, recognized him at once and called him by name. It seems that he was the man who had originally written Boswell, and having found his horses he had neglected to inform him. Thus, when he came to town four months afterward, he got snatched. You not only have to call the officer's attention to a larceny in this country, but it is absolutely necessary that you call off the sleuth hound of eternal justice when you have found the property, or you will be gathered in unless you can identify yourself. Boswell's initials are N. K., and now the boys call him Nemesis K. Boswell.

LET BALDHEADED MEN REJOICE.

THE London *Lancet* upsets the popular theory that abundant hair is a sign of bodily or mental strength. The fact is, it says, that notwithstanding the Samson precedent, the Chinese, who are the most enduring of all races, are mostly bald; and as to the supposition that long and thick hair is a sign of intellectuality, all antiquity, all madhouses and all common observation are against it. The easily-wheedled Esau was hairy. The mighty Caesar was bald. Long haired men are generally weak and fanatical, and men with scant hair are the philosophers, and soldiers, and statesmen, of the world. Oscar Wilde, Theodore Tilton, and others of the long-haired fraternity, should read these statements with soulful and heart-yearning delight.

Will the editor of the *Lancet* please step over to the saloon, opposite the royal palace, and take something at our expense? Pard, we shake with you. Count us in also. Reckon us along with Cæsar, and Elijah, and Aristotle, please. Though young, we can show more polished intellect to the superficial foot than many who have lived longer than we have.

Will the editor of the *Lancet* please put our name on his list of subscribers and send the bill to us? What we want is a good, live paper that knows something, and isn't afraid to say it.

FIRMNESS.

W E were pained to see a large mule brought into town yesterday with his side worn away until it looked very thin. It looked as though the pensive mule had laid down to think over his past life, and being in the company of seven other able-bodied mules, all of whom were attached to a government freight wagon going down a mountain, this, particular animal, while wrapped in a brown study, had been pulled several miles with so much unction, as it were, that when the train stopped it was found that this large and highly accomplished mule had worn his side off so thin that you could see his inmost thoughts.

When we saw him, he looked as though, if he had his life to live over again, he would select a different time to ponder over his previous history. Sometimes a mule's firmness causes his teetotal and everlasting overthrow.

Firmness is a good thing in its place, but we should early learn that to be firm, we need not stand up against a cyclone till our eternal economy is blown into the tops of the neighboring trees. Moral courage is a good thing, but it is useless unless you have a liver to go along with it. Sometimes a man is required to lay down his life for his principles, but the cases where he is expected to lay down his digester on the altar of his belief, are comparatively seldom.

We may often learn a valuable lesson from the stubborn mule, and guard against the too protruberant use of our own ideas in opposition to other powers against which it is useless to contend. It may be wrong for giant powder to blow the top of a man's head off without cause, but repealed contests have proved that even when giant powder is in the wrong, it is eventually victorious.

Let us, therefore, while reasonably fixed in our purpose, avoid the display of a degree of firmness which will scatter us around over two school districts, and confuse the coroner in his inquest.

PUT IN A SUMP.

THE president of the North Park and Vandaliar Mining Company not long ago got a letter from the superintendent which closed by saying that everything was working splendidly. The ore body was increasing, and the quality and richness of the rock improving with every foot. He also added that he had constructed a sump in the mine.

The president having spent most of his life in military and political affairs, had never found it necessary to use a sump, and so he didn't know to a dead moral certainty what it was that the superintendent had put in.

He hoped, however, that the expense would not cripple the company, and that by handling it carefully, they might escape damage from an explosion of the sump at an unlooked-for time.

He proceeded, however, to examine the unabridged, and found that it meant a cistern, which is constructed at the bottom of a mine for the purpose of collecting the water, and from which it is pumped.

The president, having posted himself, concluded to go and have a little conversation with one of the directors, who is a druggist in the city, and see if he knew the nature of a sump.

The president, in answer to the questions of the director relative to the latest news from the mine, said that it was looking better all the time, and that the superintendent had constructed a sump.

The director never blinked his eye. He acted like a man who has lived on sumps all his life.

"Do you know what a sump is?" asked the president. "Why, of course, anybody knows what a sump is. It's the place where they collect water from a mine, and pump it from, to free the mine from water. A man who don't know what a sump is, don't know his business, that's all I've got to say."

The president looked hurt about something. He hadn't looked for the conversation to assume just exactly the shape that it had. Finally he said, "Well you needn't point your withering sarcasm at me. I know what a sump is. I just wanted to see whether a man who had been in the pill business all his life, knew what a sump was. I knew you claimed to know almost everything, but I didn't believe you was up on that word. Now, if it's a proper question, I'd like to know just how long you have been so all-fired fluent about mining terms."

Then the director said that there was no use in putting on airs, and swelling up with pride over a little thing like that. He, for one, didn't propose to crow over other men who had not had the advantages that he had, and he would be frank with the president, and admit that an hour ago he didn't know the difference between a sump and a certiorari.

It seems that a passenger, who had come in on the same coach that brought in the superintendent's letter, had casually dropped the remark to the director that Smith had put a sump in the "Endomile," and the director had lit out for a dictionary without loss of time, so that when the two great miners got together, they were both proud and confident. Each was proud because he knew what a sump was, and confident that the other one didn't know.

MINING AS A SCIENCE.

THE study of mining as a science is one which brings with it a quiet joy, which the novice knows nothing of. In Morrison's Mining Eights we find the following:

"If all classes of lode deposits are to be regarded as legally identical, it follows that where a vein is pinched for a considerable distance, it is lost to the owner; if its apex is found in the slide, it can not be located as a lode.

"The distinction which would relieve these points would be to allow the dip to such lodes Only as have a *perpendicular base* and are not on the nature of *stratigraphical deposits!* all the inconsistencies apparent from the previous paragraph are the sequence to any other ruling.

"If it be alleged that such holdings are not applicable to fissure veins, at once a distinction is made between the two classes of veins in their consideration under the act; and if a single distinction in their legal status be admitted, no reason can be alleged against further distinctions with reference to their essential points at difference."

How, few who have not toiled over the long and wearisome works upon mining as a legal branch of human knowledge, would care a cold, dead clam, whether such lodes as have perpendicular bases, or those which have stratigraphical deposits, are to be allowed under the law in relation to pinched out or intersecting veins.

But to the student, whose whole life is wrapped up in the investigation of this beautiful mystery, these logical sequences break upon his mind with a beautiful effulgence that fills him with unstratified and purely igneous or nomicaseous joy.

Reading farther in the thrilling work, above referred to, we find this little garland of fragrant literary wood violets:

"Another point to be guarded against in the conveyance of a segregated portion of a claim on a fissure vein, is, that a line drawn at right angles to the side lines at the surface, and which is intended as the dividing fine between the part retained and the part sold, may, when carried vertically downward, cut off the vein on its dip in such a way as to divide it, for instance, at the surface. It begins 'at the west end of discovery shaft,' it may leave the bottom of such shaft entirely in the west fraction of the lode within a comparatively few feet of sinking. Such result, or a similar result, will invariably occur where the vein has a dip, unless the end lines are at an exact right angle to the strike of the vein."

Now, however, supposing that, for the sake of argument, the above be true; but, in addition thereto, a segregation of non-metallic vertically heterogeneous quartzite in non-conformity to presupposed notions of horizontal deposits of mineral in place should be agatized and truncated with diverging lines meeting at the point of intersection and disappearing with the pinched veins or departing from known proximity in company with the dividends, we have then to consider whether a winze coming in at this juncture and pinching out the assessments, would thereby invalidate tertiary flux, and thereby, in the light of a close legal examination of the slide, bar out the placer or riparian rights of contesting parties, or, if so, why in thunder should it not, or at least, what could be done about it in case the same or a totally different set of surrounding circumstances should or should not take place?

DRAWBACKS OF ROYALTY.

IT seems from our late dispatches that the prevailing assassin has made his appearance in England, and has fired at Her Royal Tallness, the Queen. The dispatch does not say why the man fired at Victoria, but the chances are that she at some time in a careless moment refused him the appointment of Book-keeper to the Queen's Livery Stable Extraordinary, or neglected to confirm his nomination to the position as Usher Plenipotentiary to the Royal Bath Room and Knight of the Queen's Cuspidor.

Royalty gets it in the nose every day or two, and yet after the family has hung onto the salary for several centuries it does not occur to the average king that he could strike a job as humorist on some London paper, at about the same salary and with none of the annoyances. The most of those people who have worn a great, heavy cast iron crown, with diamonds on it as big as a peanut, have become so attached to it that they can't swear off in a moment.

We do not see where the orchestra comes in on a thing like that. The average American would rather sell mining stock, and get wealthy without a tail on his name and his hair all worn off with a crown two sizes too large for him, than to be King of the Cannibal Islands with a missionary baby on toast twice a day.

ENGLISH HUMOR.

THE London *Spectator* says that "the humor of the United States, if closely examined, will be found to depend in a great measure on the ascendancy which the principle of utility has gained over the imaginations of a rather imaginative people." The humor of England, if closely examined, will be found just about ready to drop over the picket fence into the arena, but never quite making connections. If we scan the English literary horizon, we will find the humorist up a tall tree, depending from a sharp knot thereof by the slack of his overalls. He is just out of sight at the time you look in that direction. He always has a man working in his place, however. The man who works in his place is just paring down the half sole, and newly pegging a joke, that has recently been sent in by the foreman for repairs.

ABOUT THE AUTOPSY.

WE have been carefully reading and investigating the report of Dr. Lamb, relative to the anatomical condition of the late remnants of Charles J. Gluiteau, and also a partial or minority report furnished by the other two doctors, who got on their ear at the time of the autopsy. We are permitted to print the fragment of a private letter addressed personally to the editor from one of these gentlemen, whose name we are not permitted to use. He says:

"We found the late lamented, and after looking him over thoroughly, and removing what works he had inside of him, agreed, almost at once, that he was dead. This was the only point upon which we agreed.

"Shortly after we began to remove the internal economy of the deceased, some little discussion arose between Doc Lamb and myself about the extravasation of blood in the right pectoralis and the peculiar position of the dewflicker on the dome of the diaphragm. I made a suggestion about the causes that had led to this, stating, in my opinion, the pericarditis had crossed the median line and congested the dewdad.

"He said it was no such thing, and that I didn't know the difference between a malpighian capsule and an abdominal viscera.

"That insulted me, but I held my temper, going on with my work, removing the gall-bladder and other things, as though nothing had been said.

"By and by, Lamb said I'd better quit fooling with the pancreas, and come and help him. Then he advanced a tom-fool theory about an adhesion of the dura mater to the jib-boom, or some medical rot or other, and I told him that I thought he was wrong, and I didn't believe deceased had any dura mater. Lamb flared up then, and struck at me with a bloody towel. I then grabbed a fragment of liver, and pasted him in the nose. I don't allow any sawbone upstart to impose on me, if I know it. He then called me a very opprobrious epithet, indeed, and struck me in the eye with a kidney. Then the fight became disgraceful, and by the time we got through, the late lamented was considerably scattered. Here lay a second-hand lobe of liver, while over there was the apex of a lung hanging on a gas fixture. It was a pretty lively scrimmage, and made quite a feeling between us. I still think, however, that I was right in standing up for my theory, and when an old pelican like Lamb thinks he can scare me into St. Vitus' dance, he fools himself. The fact is, he don't know a gall-bladder from the gout, and he couldn't tell a lobulated tumor from the side of a house. I told him so, too, while I was putting some court plaster on my nose, after he pasted me with an old prison bedstead. Lamb would get along better with me if he would curb his violent temper. I guess he thought so, too, when I broke his false teeth and jammed them so far back into his oesophagus that he got blue in the face. I never allow a secondhand horse doctor to impose on me, if I know it, and it is time Doc Lamb took a grand aborescent tumble to himself."

A FEW CALM WORDS.

A LONDON paper tells how when a certain Dean of Chester was all ready to perform a marriage between persons of high standing, the bride was very late. When she reached the altar, to the question, "Wilt thou take this man?" she replied in most distinct tones, "I will not." On retiring with the Dean to the vestry, she explained that her late arrival was not her fault, and that the bridegroom had accosted her on her arrival at the church with, "G—d d——n you, if this is the way you begin you'll find it to to your cost when you're my wife."

That was no way to open up a honeymoon. They are not doing that way recently, and in the bon ton and dishabille select and etcetera society of the more metropolitan cities, such a remark would at once be considered as outre and Corpus Christi.

The groom should stop and consider that sometimes the most annoying accidents occur to a young lady in dressing. Suppose for instance that in stooping over to button her shoe she breaks a spoke in her corset and has to send it to the blacksmith shop, do you think that the groom is justified in kicking over the altar and dragging his affianced up the aisle by the hair of the head? We would rather suggest that he would not. There are other distressing accidents which may happen at such a time to the prospective bride, but we forbear to enter into the harrowing details. No man with the finer feelings of a gentleman will ever knock his new wife down in the church and tramp on her, until he knows to a reasonable degree of certainty that he is right. It may be annoying, of course, to the groom to stand and look out of the window for half an hour while the bride is allaying the hemorrhage of a pimple on her nose with a powder puff, but then, great hemlock! if a man can't endure that and smile, how will he behave when the clothesline falls down and the baby gets a kernel of corn up its nose?

These are questions which naturally occur to the candid and thinking mind and command our attention. The groom who would swear at his wife for being a few minutes late at the altar, would kill her and throw her stiffened remains over into the sheep corral if she allowed the twins to eat crackers in his bed and scatter the crumbs over his couch.

Let us look these matters calmly in the face, and not allow ourselves to drift away into space.

DON'T LIKE OUR STYLE.

OSCAR WILDE closes his remarks about America thus: "But it is in the decay of manners that the thoughtful and well-bred American has cause for regret. I have repeatedly said this, but I am told in reply: 'We are still a young country, and you must not be too severe upon us.' 'Yes,' I answer, 'but when your country was still younger, it's manners were better. They have never been equal since to what they were in Washington's time, a man whose manners were irreproachable. I believe a most serious problem for the American people to consider, is the cultivation of better manners among its people. It is the most noticeable, the most painful defect in American civilization." Yes, Oscar, you are, in a measure, correct. Our manners are a little decayed. So also were the eggs with which you were greeted in some of our cities. That may have given you a wrong impression as to our manners and their state of health. We just want to straighten out any little error of judgment on your part as to American customs, and to impress upon your mind the fact that the decayed article which, in most cases you considered our miasma-impregnated etiquette, was what is known among savants as decayed cabbage.

MR. T. WILSON.

THE gentleman above referred to has accomplished one of the most remarkable feats known to modern science. Though uneducated, and perhaps inexperienced, he has attracted toward himself the notice of the world.

Though he was once a poor boy, unnoticed and unknown, he has risen to the proud eminence from which, with pride, and covered with glory and sore places, he may survey the civilized world. He entered upon an argument with Mr. Sullivan, knowing the mental strength and powers of his adversary, and yet he never flinched. He stood up before his powerful antagonist, and acquired a national reputation, and a large octagonal breadth of black and blue intellect, which are the envy and admiration of 50,000,000 people.

This should be a convincing argument to our growing youth of the possibilities in store for the earnest, untiring and enthusiastic thumper. It is an example of the wonderful triumph of mind over matter. It shows how certain intellectual developments may be acquired almost instantaneously. It demonstrates at once that phrenological protuberances may be grown more rapidly and more spontaneously than the scientist has ever been willing to admit.

A few weeks ago, Tug Wilson was as obscure as the greenback party. Now he is known from ocean to ocean, and his fame is as universal as is that of Dr. Tanner, the starvation prima donna of the world. Few men have the intellectual stamina to withstand the strain of such an argument as he did, but he left the arena with a collection of knobs and arnica clustering around his brow, which he justly merited, and the world will not grudge him this meagre acquisition. It was due to his own exertions and his own prowess, and there is no American so mean as to wrest it from him.

Thousands of our own boys, who to-day are spearing frogs, or bathing in the rivers of their native land and parading on the shingly beach with no clothes on to speak of, are left to choose between such a career of usefulness and greatness of brow, and the hum-drum life of a bilious student and pale, sad congressman. Will you rise to the proud pinnacle of fame as a pugilist, boys, or will you plug along as a sorrowing, overworked statesman? Now, in the spring-time of your lives, choose between the two, and abide the consequences.

ETIQUETTE OF THE NAPKIN.

IT has been stated, and very truly too, that the law of the napkin is but vaguely understood It may be said, however, on the start, that custom and good breeding have uttered the decree that it is in poor taste to put the napkin in the pocket and carry it away.

The rule of etiquette is becoming more and more thoroughly established, that the napkin should be left at the house of the host or hostess, after dinner.

There has been a good deal of discussion, also, upon the matter of folding the napkin after dinner, and whether it should be so disposed of, or negligently tossed into the gravy boat. If, however, it can be folded easily, and without attracting too much attention and prolonging the session for several hours, it should be so arranged, and placed beside the plate, where it may be easily found by the hostess, and returned to her neighbor from whom she borrowed it for the occasion. If, however, the lady of the house is not doing her own work, the napkin may be carefully jammed into a globular wad, and fired under the table, to convey the idea of utter recklessness and pampered abandon.

The use of the finger bowl is also a subject of much importance to the bon ton guest who gorges himself at the expense of his friends.

The custom of drinking out of the finger bowl, though not entirely obsolete, has been limited to the extent that good breeding does not now permit the guest to quaff the water from his finger howl, unless he does so prior to using it as a finger bowl.

Thus it will be seen that social customs are slowly but surely cutting down and circumscribing the rights and privileges of the masses.

At the court of Eugenie, the customs of the table were very rigid, and the most prominent guest of H. R. H. was liable to get the G. B. if he spread his napkin on his lap, and cut his egg in two with a carving knife. The custom was that the napkin should be hung on one knee, and the egg busted at the big end and scooped out with a spoon.

A prominent American, at her table, one day, in an unguarded moment, shattered the shell of a soft-boiled egg with his knife, and, while prying it apart, both thumbs were erroneously jammed into the true inwardness of the fruit with so much momentum that the juice took him in the eye, thus blinding him and maddening him to such a degree, that he got up and threw the remnants into the bosom of the hired man plenipotentiary, who stood near the table, scratching his ear with a tray. As may readily be supposed, there was a painful interim during which it was hard to tell for five or six minutes whether the prominent American or the hired man would come out on top; but at last the American, with the egg in his eye, got the ear of the high-priced hired man in among his back teeth, and the honor of our beloved flag was vindicated.

AN INFERNAL MACHINE.

A SINGULAR thing occurred in England the other day, and in view of its truth, and also in order that the American side of the affair may be shown in the correct light, we give the facts as they occurred, having obtained our information directly from the parties who were implicated in the affair. We hesitate to take hold of the subject, but our duty to the American people demands some action, and we do not falter.

During the past winter there arrived in London a suspicious-looking metallic box, with a peculiar thumb-screw or button on the top. It was sent by mail, and was addressed to a prominent land owner. This gentleman had been on the watch for some explosive machine for some time, and when it was brought to him, he at once turned it over to the authorities for investigation. The police force, detective force and chemists were called in, and requested to ascertain the nature of the infernal machine, and, if possible, where it came from.

Experts examined the box, and, with the aid of a cord attached to the suspicious button on top, pulled open the metallic box without explosion. The substance contained therein, was of a dark color, with a strong smell of ammonia. All kinds of tests were made by the experts, in order to ascertain of what kind of combustible it was composed. The odor was carefully noted, as well as the taste, and then there was a careful chemical analysis made, which was barren of result. In the midst of the general alarm, the London papers, with large scare-heads and astonishers, gave full and elaborate reports of the attempt upon the life of a prominent man, through the agency of a new and very peculiar machine, loaded with an explosive, of which scientists could gain no knowledge or information whatever.

It looked as though the assassin was far in advance of science, or at least of professional chemists, and the matter was about to be given up in despair, when the following letter arrived from San Antonio, Texas, United States of America:

"My Dear Sir:—I sent you by a recent mail, prepaid, a small metallic box of bat guano, from the caves of Texas, for analysis and experiment. Please acknowledge receipt of saine.

"Morton Frewen."

Then the experts went home. They felt as though science had done all it could in this case, and they needed rest, and perfect calm, and change of scene. They hadn't seen their families for some time, and they wanted to go home and get acquainted with their wives. They didn't ask for any pay for their services. They just said it was in the interest of science, and they couldn't have the heart to charge anything for it. One chemist started off without his umbrella, and never went back after it.

When he got home he was troubled with nausea, and they had to feed him on cracker toast for several weeks.

We tell this incident simply to vindicate America. The London papers did not give all the proceedings, and we feel it our duty to place the United States upon a square footing with England in this matter. Of course it is a little tough on the experts, but when we know our duty to our magnificent country and the land that gave us birth, there is no earthly power we fear, no terrestrial snoozer who can deter us from its performance.

THE CODFISH.

THIS tropical bird very seldom wings his way so far west as Wyoming. He loves the sea breezes and humid atmosphere of the Atlantic ocean, and when isolated in this mountain clime, pines for his native home.

The codfish cannot sing, but is prized for his beautiful plumage and seductive odor.

The codfish of commerce is devoid of digestive apparatus, and is more or less permeated with salt.

Codfish on toast is not as expensive as quail on toast.

The codfish ball is made of the shattered remains of the adult codfish, mixed with the tropical Irish potato of commerce.

The codfish has a great wealth of glad, unfettered smile. When he laughs at anything, he has that same wide waste of mirth and back teeth that Mr. Talmage has. The Wyoming codfish is generally dead. Death, in most cases, is the result of exposure and loss of appetite. No one can look at the codfish of commerce, and not shed a tear. Far from home, with his system filled with salt, while his internal economy is gone, there is an air of sadness and homesickness and briny hopelessness about him that no one can see unmoved.

It is in our home life, however, that the codfish makes himself felt and remembered. When he enters our household, we feel his all pervading presence, like the perfume of wood violets, or the seductive odor of a dead mouse in the piano.

Friends may visit us and go away, to be forgotten with the advent of a new face; but the cold, calm, silent corpse of the codfish cannot be forgotten. Its chastened influence permeates the entire ranch. It steals into the parlor, like an unbidden guest, and flavors the costly curtains and the high-priced lambrequins. It enters the dark closet and dallies lovingly with your swallowtail coat. It goes into your sleeping apartment, and makes its home in your glove box and your handkerchief case.

That is why we say that it is a solemn thing to take the life of a codfish. We would not do it. We would pass him by, a thousand times, no matter how ferocious he might be, rather than take his life, and have our once happy home haunted forever by his unholy presence.

HIS AGED MOTHER.

AN exchange says that "the James boys had a morose and ugly disposition." This may be regarded as authentic. The James boys were not only morose, but they were at times irritable and even boorish. Some of their acts would seem to savor of the most coarse and rude of impulses. Jesse James at different times killed over fifty men. This would show that his disposition must have been soured by some great sorrow. A person who fills the New Jerusalem with people, or kills a majority of the republican voters of a precinct, or the entire board of directors of a national bank, or who remorselessly kills all the first-class passengers on a through train, just because he feels crochety and disagreeable, must be morose and sullen in his disposition. No man, who is healthy and full of animal spirits, could massacre the ablebodied voters of a whole village, unless he felt cross and taciturn naturally.

There should have been a post mortem examination of Mr. James to determine what was the matter with him. We were in favor of a post mortem examination of Mr. James twelve years ago, but there seemed to be a feeling of reluctance on the part of the authorities about holding it. No one seemed to doubt the propriety of such a movement, but there was a kind of vague hesitation by the proper officials on account of his mother. There has been a vast amount of thoughtfulness manifested by the Missouri people on behalf of Jesse's mother. For nearly twenty years they have put off the post mortem examination of Mr. James, because they knew that his mother would feel wretched and gloomy when she saw her son with his vitals in one market basket, and his vertebræ in another. The American people hate like sin to step in between a mother and her child, and create unpleasant sensations.

Mr. Pinkerton was the most considerate. At first he said he would hold an autopsy on Mr. James right away, but it consumed so much time holding autopsies on his detectives, that he postponed Jesse's post mortem for a long time. He also hoped that after the lapse of years, may be, Mr. James would become enfeebled so that he could steal up behind him, some night, and stun him with a Chicago pie; but Jesse seemed vigorous, up to a late date, and out of respect for his aged mother, the Chicago sleuth hounds of justice have spared him.

Detectives are sometimes considered hardhearted and unloving in their natures, but this is not the case. Very few of them can bear to witness the shedding of blood, especially their own blood. Sometimes they find it necessary to kill a man in order to restore peace to the country, but they very rarely kill a man like James. This is partly due to the fact that they hate to cut a man like that right down, before he has a chance to repent. They are prone to give him probation, and yet another chance to turn. Still, there are lots of mean, harsh, unthinking people who do not give the detectives credit for this.

BUSINESS LETTERS.

ALL business letters, as a rule, demand some kind of an answer, especially those containing money. To neglect the reply to a letter is an insult, unless the letter failed to contain a stamp. In your reply, first acknowledge the receipt of the letter, then the receipt of the money, whatever it is.

Letters asking for money or the payment of a bill, may be postponed from time to time if necessary. No man should reply to such a letter while angry. If the amount is small and you are moderately hot, wait two days. If the sum is quite large and you are tempted to write an insulting letter, wait two weeks, or until you have thoroughly cooled down.

Business letters should be written on plain, neat paper, with your name and business neatly printed at the top by the Boomekang job printer.

Letters from railroad companies referring to important improvements, etc., etc., should contain pass, not for publication, but as a guarantee of good faith.

Neat and beautiful penmanship is very desirable in business correspondence, but it is most important that you should not spell God with a little g or codfish with a k. Ornamental penmanship is good, but it will not take the cuss off if you don't know how to spell.

Read your letter over carefully after you have written it, if you can; if not, send it with an apology about the rush of business.

In ordering goods, state whether you will remit soon or whether the account should be placed in the refrigerator.

DANGER OF GARDENING.

A COLORADO book agent writes us about as follows: "For some time past it has been my desire to insure my life for the benefit of my family, but I knew the public sentiment so well that I feared it could not be done. I knew that there was a deep and bitter enmity against book agents, which I found had pervaded the insurance world to such an extent that I would be unable to obtain insurance at a reasonable premium.

"The popular belief is that book agents are shot on sight and their mangled bodies thrown into the tall grass or fed to the coyotes.

"I found, however, that I could get my life insured for two thousand dollars by paying a premium of twelve dollars per year, as a book agent. This was far better than anything I had ever looked for. The question arose as to whether I worked in my garden or not, and I was forced to admit that I did. It ought to reduce the premium if a man works in his garden, and thus, by short periods of vigorous exercise, prolongs his life, but it don't seem to be that way. They charged me an additional three dollars on the premium, because I toiled a little among my pet rutabagas.

"I don't know what the theory is about this matter. Perhaps the company labors under the impression that a thousand-legged worm might crawl into my ear and kill me, or a purple-top turnip might explode and knock my brains out.

"Of course, in the midst of life we are in death, but I always used to think I was safer mashing my squash-bugs and hoeing my blue-eyed beans than when I was on the road, dodging bulldogs and selling books.

"Perhaps some amateur gardener, in a careless moment, at some time or other, has been stabbed in the diaphragm by a murderous radish, or a watermelon may have stolen up to some man, in years gone by, and brained him with part of a picket fence. There must be statistics somewhere by which the insurance companies have arrived at this high rate on gardeners. If you know anything of this matter, I wish you would write me, for if hoeing sweet corn and cultivating string beans is going to sock me into an early grave I want to know it."

Lector House believes that a society develops through a two-fold approach of continuous learning and adaptation, which is derived from the study of classic literary works spread across the historic timeline of literature records. Therefore, we aim at reviving, repairing and redeveloping all those inaccessible or damaged but historically as well as culturally important literature across subjects so that the future generations may have an opportunity to study and learn from past works to embark upon a journey of creating a better future.

This book is a result of an effort made by Lector House towards making a contribution to the preservation and repair of original ancient works which might hold historical significance to the approach of continuous learning across subjects.

HAPPY READING & LEARNING!

LECTOR HOUSE LLP
E-MAIL: lectorpublishing@gmail.com